Southern Scrumptious

Favorites

BY BETTY SIMS

*I dedicate this book to our son,
William Arthur "Bill" Sims Jr., who lost his battle against
amyotrophic lateral sclerosis (Lou Gehrig's disease)
on Friday, July 13, 2007. Bill loved life and
lived it to the fullest until his death.*

The purchase of this book will help my family's quest to find a cure for ALS.
The Community Foundation of Middle Tennessee
Sims Family ALS Research Fund
3833 Cleghorn Avenue #400, Nashville, Tennessee 37215-2519

Southern Scrumptious Favorites

Published by Scrumptious, Inc.
Copyright © 2011 by Betty Brandon Sims
4107 Indian Hills Road, Decatur, Alabama 35603
mettysims@aol.com   www.scrumptiousinc.com

Cover Artwork © by Lisa Sims Wallace
Illustrations © by Libby Sims Patrick

Library of Congress Control Number: 2010932338
ISBN: 978-0-9659053-2-9

Edited, Designed, and Produced by

 Favorite Recipes® Press

An imprint of

FRP.INC

A wholly owned subsidiary of Southwestern/Great American, Inc.
P.O. Box 305142, Nashville, Tennessee 37230
1-800-358-0560

Project Editor: Tanis Westbrook
Series Designers: Bill Kersey and David Malone
Art Director and Book Design: Steve Newman

Manufactured in the United States of America
First Printing: 2011
5,000 copies

Acknowledgments

Thank you, dear family, for the love, support and good times you have given me and the courage with which you have faced life under many adversities, always with smiles, laughter, and hope for the future. You know, "Laughter is the best medicine."—William Shakespeare

Cover Illustrations: Lisa Sims Wallace
Lisa has painted for most of her life and began selling her artwork in 1990. She, her husband, Paul, and sons live in Florence, Alabama. She loves living in Alabama for the inspiration so readily available around her every day. You can find her on the Web at www.lisawallace.com.

Line Drawings: Libby Sims Patrick, IIDA
Libby is an award-winning interior designer who loves to draw. Her firm, Sims Patrick Studios, Inc., specializes in commercial and residential projects. She is my oldest daughter and lives with her husband, Carl, and son, Alex, in Atlanta, Georgia. Her Web site is www.simspatrickstudio.com.

Sheryl Sims Hofherr
Sheryl earned a (BS) Bachelor of Science in public relations and journalism from Auburn University. She has been so helpful with proofreading. She lives with her children, Brandon and Finlay, in Atlanta, Georgia.

Contents

Contents

Introduction

The special recipes contained in *Southern Scrumptious Favorites* are the tried and true recipes presented in Scrumptious Cooking School during the last few years. We have had so much fun preparing these recipes with our wonderful classes. I have had fabulous assistance from the darling and efficient Nicole Shelton; Greg Clemons, CPA, a great cook as well as being a great guy; Cherri Carr, who types our menus and is my friend and "girl Friday;" and Jo Hosey, who is always willing to "spruce up" my house for any occasion with her lovely arrangements. Recently, I have launched some products for ALS research, and my longtime friend Margaret Minton has been such a help with these. There are ten menus in the front of the book with recipes and directions to execute each event. In the back are many more recipes you will love, and you may want to substitute some of these into the menus. Also check the back of the book for guides in planning your event.

I grew up with a passion for cooking in the small town of Cartersville, Georgia. My mom was an excellent cook and loved having me in the kitchen with her. When I was twelve years old, I started a small business of making cakes for Mother and Dad's friends for birthdays and parties. Mom gave me the ingredients so I made full profit for my allowance. I think she believed this would encourage me to stay busy and out of trouble. My friends would come over to lick icing bowls and then we would do the things kids generally do.

After spending four years majoring in Foods and Nutrition at the University of Tennessee, I met and married Bill Sims, who was in medical school preparing to become an orthopedic surgeon. Together we raised four children—all born within a five-year span—so we essentially raised them as a litter. We led a very busy life after we established residence in Decatur, Alabama. When our youngest daughter left for college, I decided to open Johnston Street Café, which I kept for ten years. Next came Scrumptious Culinary School, two cookbooks, traveling to teach cooking classes, and various speaking engagements and book signings.

I guess I have fulfilled the prophesy of feature writer Eunice Ginn Adams in Cartersville, Georgia, who wrote about me for *The Tribune News* when I was twelve. "Today excellent cooks are known far and wide and rewarded for their skill in various ways. One of the youngest cooks in Cartersville, whose skill is well-known outside the family circle, is Betty Brandon, 12-year-old daughter of Professor and Mrs. W. H. Brandon. Her first love and specialty is cake baking and her Christmas present from her parents was not a brooch but a far more practical gift, a Mixmaster, which has saved Betty a great deal of hard beating of batter for the delicious cakes of all varieties which she makes weekly."

This is the third of my own cookbooks—*Southern Scrumptious: How to Cater Your Own Party, Southern Scrumptious Entertains,* and now *Southern Scrumptious Favorites.* I co-edited *Cotton Country Cooking* for Decatur Junior Service League with my dear friend Katherine Wilks years ago. Who knows what will come next? Happy Cooking!

An Elegant Brunch

Menu

Everyday Granola

Skillet Coffee Cake

Granola Parfait

Cream Drop Biscuits

Grits Soufflé

Cheesy Hash Brown Casserole

Mimosas

One of my favorite ways to entertain is a mid-morning brunch shared with family or friends on a leisurely Saturday or Sunday morning. If you want an elegant or formal look, use your very best china and wrap the silverware in linen napkins with silver or gold ribbon. For a more casual feel, use decorative paper plates and tie napkins with raffia. Set up your water and mimosa bar so refreshments will be ready to pass as soon as your guests arrive. Serve two to four options of fruit juices in crystal pitchers alongside Champagne chilling in buckets, plenty of flutes, and whole berries or sliced fruits for garnish. Interesting options include blackberry or raspberry, mango, blood orange, and cherry juices. The day before your brunch, prepare the Cheesy Hash Brown Casserole, the fruit, and the Skillet Coffee Cake. The morning of your event, assemble the yogurt parfait. Buy or make your own granola. Use the prettiest martini glasses or stemmed dessert dishes for your parfaits. The layers of yogurt, granola, and fruit show up best in crystal containers. Stir up the Cream Drop Biscuits, or you can purchase the delicious Sister Schubert Orange Rolls (many other varieties also are available) and keep them in the freezer for any occasion. Stir up the Grits Soufflé and bake just before serving. You actually can make it up the day before, refrigerate, and remove from the refrigerator an hour before baking. Don't forget the flavored butters or jams for the biscuits. A lineup for your buffet should be: napkin-wrapped silverware, plates, parfaits, casserole, grits, coffee cake, biscuits, and butters.

Everyday Granola

3 cups old-fashioned oats

1 cup coarsely chopped
    pecans

1/2 cup unsweetened
    shredded coconut

3 tablespoons brown sugar

3/4 teaspoon ground
    cinnamon

1/2 teaspoon ground ginger

1/4 teaspoon (heaping) salt

1/3 cup honey

2 tablespoons vegetable oil

1 cup assorted dried fruit

Combine the oats, pecans, coconut, brown sugar, cinnamon, ginger and salt in a large bowl and mix well. Heat the honey and oil in a saucepan over medium-low heat until smooth, stirring constantly. Add to the oat mixture and toss to coat. Spread on a rimmed baking sheet lined with baking parchment. Bake at 300 degrees for 40 minutes or until golden brown, stirring every 10 minutes. Remove to a wire rack. Stir and let stand until cool. Stir in the dried fruit. Store in an airtight container for up to three weeks.

Yield: about 5 cups

Skillet Coffee Cake

Dense and slightly almond-flavored, this cake is "to die for." When we tested this for Cotton Country Cooking *we all loved it. It freezes well.*

3/4 cup (11/2 sticks) butter or
    margarine, melted

11/2 cups sugar

2 eggs

11/2 cups sifted
    all-purpose flour

Pinch of salt

1 teaspoon almond extract

Slivered almonds

Sugar for sprinkling

Line a 9- or 11-inch cast-iron skillet with foil, leaving an overhang on the side. Combine the butter and 11/2 cups sugar in a mixing bowl and mix well. Beat in the eggs one at a time. Add the flour, salt and almond extract and mix well. Pour into the prepared skillet. Cover the top with slivered almonds and sprinkle with sugar. Bake at 350 degrees for 30 to 40 minutes or until the coffee cake tests done. Lift the coffee cake from the skillet using the foil overhang and place on a wire rack to cool. Wrap tightly in the foil to store. Do not try to remove the foil while the coffee cake is still warm because it will stick.

Yield: 8 servings

Granola Parfait

4 cups Everyday Granola
    (at left)

8 cups vanilla yogurt

4 cups sliced strawberries

11/2 cups blueberries

Place 1/4 cup granola in the bottom of each parfait or martini glass. Add 1/2 cup yogurt and 1/4 cup strawberries. Sprinkle with some of the blueberries. Repeat the layers, ending with the blueberries.

Yield: 8 servings

Cream Drop Biscuits

2 1/2 cups all-purpose flour
1 tablespoon baking
  powder
1 teaspoon salt
1 tablespoon sugar
2 cups heavy cream,
  chilled

Mix the flour, baking
powder, salt and sugar
in a large bowl. Add the
cream and stir to form a
soft dough. Drop by
heaping 1/4 cupfuls 1 inch
apart onto an ungreased
large baking sheet. Bake
at 400 degrees on the
middle oven rack for
18 to 20 minutes or until
the tops are pale golden
brown and the bottoms are
golden brown.

Yield: 8 servings

Grits Soufflé

Who doesn't like grits in the South? We are converting many Northerners to "grits eaters." I prefer to cook the grits in milk, which makes them creamier.

1/2 cup (1 stick) unsalted
  butter
3 cups water
1 teaspoon salt
2 cups quick-cooking grits
3 cups milk
1 tablespoon sugar
2 cups (8 ounces) shredded
  Swiss cheese
1 red bell pepper, seeded
  and chopped
1 jalapeño chile, seeded
  and chopped
Kernels from 2 ears of fresh
  corn, or 1 cup fresh or
  frozen corn kernels
4 eggs, lightly beaten
1 tablespoon fresh thyme, or
  1 teaspoon dried thyme
2 teaspoons salt
1/2 teaspoon freshly
  ground pepper

Butter a 3-quart soufflé dish or 9×13-inch baking dish with 2 tablespoons of the butter. Bring the water and 1 teaspoon salt to a boil in a medium saucepan. Reduce the heat to medium. Add the grits gradually in a slow steady stream, whisking constantly. Cook for 10 minutes or until thickened, stirring constantly. Add 1 1/2 cups of the milk. Cook for 5 minutes or until the milk is absorbed, stirring constantly. Remove from the heat. Stir in the remaining 1 1/2 cups milk, remaining 6 tablespoons butter and the sugar until well blended. Add the cheese, bell pepper, jalapeño chile, corn, eggs, thyme, 2 teaspoons salt and the pepper and mix well. Pour into the prepared soufflé dish. Bake at 350 degrees for 45 to 55 minutes or until the soufflé has risen, is firm around the edge and the center is slightly soft. Remove from the oven and let stand for 5 minutes before serving. Serve warm.

Yield: 8 servings

Cheesy Hash Brown Casserole

*Freeze casseroles to keep on hand for friends in need
(illness, new baby, funeral, etc.).*

1/4 cup (1/2 stick) butter
1/4 cup all-purpose flour
1 cup milk
1 cup half-and-half
4 cups (16 ounces) shredded
 sharp Cheddar cheese
1 teaspoon Italian seasoning
1/2 teaspoon pepper
12 hard-cooked eggs, sliced
8 slices pepper bacon,
 cooked and crumbled
1 (16-ounce) package frozen
 hash brown potatoes,
 thawed
4 slices whole wheat bread,
 crumbled (about 2 cups)
3 tablespoons butter, melted

Melt 1/4 cup butter in a saucepan over medium-low heat. Add the flour. Cook for 1 minute or until smooth, stirring constantly. Stir in the milk and half-and-half gradually. Cook over medium heat until thickened, stirring constantly. Add the cheese, Italian seasoning and pepper. Cook until the cheese melts, stirring constantly. Remove from the heat. Layer one-half of the egg slices, one-half of the bacon and one-half of the cheese sauce in a lightly greased 9×13-inch baking dish. Layer the hash brown potatoes over the layers. Continue layering with the remaining egg slices, bacon and cheese sauce. Combine the bread crumbs and 3 tablespoons butter in a bowl and toss to coat. Sprinkle over the top. Chill, covered, for up to 8 hours, if desired. Remove from the refrigerator and let stand for 30 minutes. Bake, uncovered, at 350 degrees for 40 to 45 minutes or until golden and bubbly.

Yield: 8 servings

Mimosas

Fill each Champagne flute halfway with fresh orange juice with no pulp. Top off with chilled Champagne.

A Special Occasion Dinner

Menu

Peach Sangria

Red and White Grape Salad

Pimm's Cup

Jumbo Lump Crab Cakes with Meyer Lemon Sauce or Mango Salsa

Creamy Wild Mushroom Risotto

Microwave Risotto

Balsamic-Glazed Brussels Sprouts

Apple Bread Pudding with Brandy Sauce

If your special dinner is in the late spring or summer months, serving sangria is appropriate. If not, more appropriate drinks include nonalcoholic punch and/or assorted wines. This dinner could be used to celebrate a birthday, anniversary, or a friend's promotion. This menu is easily executed and so delicious. The Grape Salad, Meyer Lemon Sauce, and Apple Bread Pudding can be made the day before the event and refrigerated. After coating the crab cakes with panko crumbs, they also may be covered and refrigerated the day before or the morning of the dinner. The Creamy Wild Mushroom Risotto can be made in the afternoon and reheated before guests arrive. Bacon may be fried and crumbled early in the day for the brussels sprouts. The Simses are always celebrating special occasions, and this is one menu we use often. Substitute recipes from the back of the book if, for instance, you do not care for brussels sprouts. However, this is a very tasty recipe and brussels sprouts are gaining in popularity.

Peach Sangria

2 firm-ripe peaches, cut into
    thin wedges (use frozen if
    fresh is not available)
1/2 cup peach schnapps
1/3 cup superfine sugar
3 cups chilled rosé
    (750-milliliter bottle)
2 cups chilled sparkling water
Ice

Combine the peaches, schnapps and sugar
in a large pitcher and stir until the sugar is
dissolved. Let stand for 1 hour. Stir in the
wine, sparkling water and some ice.

Yield: 4 tall drinks

Red and White Grape Salad

*This is such a heavenly salad, but it does have a few calories. Use light
cream cheese and sour cream for a lighter touch.*

8 ounces cream cheese,
    softened
1 cup sour cream
1/2 cup granulated sugar
1 teaspoon vanilla extract
2 cups red seedless grapes
2 cups white seedless grapes
1/2 cup packed brown sugar
1/2 cup chopped pecans

Mix the cream cheese, sour cream, granulated
sugar and vanilla in a bowl. Stir in the grapes.
Spoon into a serving bowl. Mix the brown
sugar and pecans in a small bowl. Sprinkle
over the grape mixture. Chill, covered, until
serving time.

Yield: 8 servings

Pimm's Cup

2 ounces Pimm's No. 1
Lemon-lime soda or
    ginger ale
Ice
Wedge of lemon or orange
Slice of cucumber

Pour the Pimm's and
lemon-lime soda into a
chilled highball glass
filled with ice. Squeeze
the lemon into the glass
and stir. Garnish with
the cucumber.

Yield: 1 serving

Jumbo Lump Crab Cakes with Meyer Lemon Sauce

This is one of my most favorite recipes. I do not add a lot of extra ingredients.

1 pound jumbo lump
    crab meat, shells removed
    and meat flaked
1 tablespoon lemon juice
3/4 cup mayonnaise
1 teaspoon salt
1/2 teaspoon ground
    white pepper
2 cups panko (Japanese
    bread crumbs)
Butter for sautéing
Meyer Lemon Sauce (below)

Combine the crab meat, lemon juice, mayonnaise, salt and white pepper in a bowl and stir gently with a rubber spatula just until mixed. Shape into 2- to 2^1/$_2$-ounce patties. Coat the patties with the panko. Sauté the patties in butter in an ovenproof skillet until golden brown and turn. Bake at 300 degrees for 10 minutes. Serve with Meyer Lemon Sauce or your favorite mango salsa.

Yield: 12 crab cakes

Meyer Lemons

If you can possibly find them, use Meyer lemons for this sauce. Most of the nurseries have these plants or trees for sale in the summer.

Meyer Lemon Sauce

1/2 cup mayonnaise
2 tablespoons fresh Meyer
    lemon juice
1^1/$_2$ teaspoons finely grated
    Meyer lemon zest
1^1/$_2$ teaspoons Dijon
    mustard
1 teaspoon sherry vinegar
1 cup extra-virgin olive oil
Salt and pepper to taste

Place the mayonnaise in a small bowl. Whisk in the lemon juice and lemon zest. Whisk in the mustard and vinegar gradually. Whisk in the olive oil gradually. Add salt and pepper. This sauce can be made a day ahead and chilled, covered, in the refrigerator. Bring to room temperature and whisk before serving.

Yield: 1^1/$_2$ cups

Creamy Wild Mushroom Risotto

Always use arborio rice for risotto as it has more starch and breaks down and becomes creamier than other rice.

2 1/2 cups chicken broth
1 cup chopped onion
1 garlic clove, crushed
2 teaspoons olive oil
1 cup uncooked arborio rice
    or other short-grain rice
1 (3-ounce) package fresh
    shiitake mushrooms, sliced
1 cup sliced fresh crimini
    mushrooms or white
    domestic mushrooms
1/4 cup (1 ounce) freshly
    grated Parmesan cheese
2 tablespoons chardonnay
    or dry white wine
Sprigs of fresh herbs
    for garnish

Bring the broth to a boil in a small saucepan. Cover and reduce the heat to low. Keep warm. Cook the onion and garlic in the olive oil in a large skillet over medium heat until the onion is tender, stirring constantly. Add the rice. Cook for 4 minutes, stirring constantly. Add the mushrooms and 1/2 cup of the warm broth. Cook until most of the broth is absorbed, stirring constantly. Repeat with the remaining broth 1/2 cup at a time until all of the broth has been absorbed, the rice is tender and the mixture is creamy. The entire process should take about 25 minutes. Stir in the cheese and wine. Spoon into a serving bowl. Garnish with sprigs of fresh herbs. Serve immediately.

Yield: 8 servings

Once we had a cooking class and it was quite large, forty or so. My assistant, Nicole Shelton, was at the stove stirring a massive amount of risotto, adding a little liquid at a time to make it creamy. She said to me, "Betty, don't ever serve this again at a cooking class." She was so hot. It's a good idea to either serve the regular risotto when you are entertaining only a few, or use the microwave version. The risotto can be partially cooked early in the day and finished just before serving when you are serving a lot of people, which is the method restaurants use.

Microwave Risotto

Preparing risotto can be labor-intensive, so use this alternative microwave method which eliminates standing over the stove while the risotto cooks.

1/4 cup (1/2 stick)
    unsalted butter
1 small yellow
    onion, chopped
1 cup dry white wine
5 1/2 cups low-sodium
    chicken broth
2 cups arborio rice
1 cup (4 ounces) grated
    Parmesan cheese
1 teaspoon kosher salt
1/2 teaspoon pepper

Place the butter and onion in a large microwave-safe bowl. Microwave on High for 5 minutes. Add the wine and broth. Microwave for 4 minutes. Stir in the rice. Microwave until the rice is cooked to desired consistency checking every 3 or 4 minutes. Stir in the cheese, salt and pepper. Let stand at room temperature for 5 minutes or until the liquid is absorbed. Stir and microwave for 2 minutes longer if needed.

Yield: 8 servings

Balsamic-Glazed Brussels Sprouts

Bill's dad called brussels sprouts "Sunday cabbage."

4 slices thick-sliced bacon
1 tablespoon minced garlic
1/2 cup balsamic vinegar
1 1/2 tablespoons sugar
3/4 teaspoon salt
1/2 teaspoon pepper
2 pounds fresh brussels
    sprouts, cut into halves

Cook the bacon in a large nonstick skillet over medium heat for 15 minutes or until brown and crisp. Remove the bacon to paper towels to drain. Crumble the bacon and set aside. Drain the skillet, reserving 1/4 cup of the bacon drippings in the skillet. Add the garlic. Cook for 1 minute. Stir in the balsamic vinegar, sugar, salt and pepper. Add the brussels sprouts and stir to coat. Cook, covered, for 5 minutes. Uncover and increase the heat to medium-high. Cook for 10 minutes, stirring frequently. Garnish with the crumbled bacon.

Yield: 8 servings

Apple Bread Pudding with Brandy Sauce

Bread puddings are great desserts for a dinner party as they can be made ahead (two days, if necessary) and chilled. This recipe is a favorite of mine, and tastes super with Brandy Sauce. We have a great apple tree at our river home.

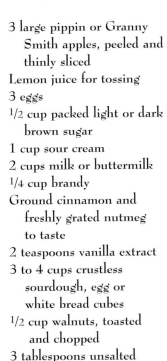

3 large pippin or Granny Smith apples, peeled and thinly sliced
Lemon juice for tossing
3 eggs
1/2 cup packed light or dark brown sugar
1 cup sour cream
2 cups milk or buttermilk
1/4 cup brandy
Ground cinnamon and freshly grated nutmeg to taste
2 teaspoons vanilla extract
3 to 4 cups crustless sourdough, egg or white bread cubes
1/2 cup walnuts, toasted and chopped
3 tablespoons unsalted butter, cut into pieces
Brown sugar for sprinkling
Brandy Sauce (below)

Toss the apples with a small amount of lemon juice in a bowl to prevent browning. Combine the eggs, 1/2 cup brown sugar, the sour cream, milk, brandy, cinnamon, nutmeg and vanilla in a large bowl and mix well. Stir in the bread cubes, apples and walnuts. Let stand for 15 minutes. Spoon into a buttered 6- or 8-cup baking dish or soufflé dish. Top with the butter. Sprinkle with brown sugar. Place the baking dish in a larger baking dish. Add enough hot water to the larger baking dish to come halfway up the sides of the smaller baking dish. Bake at 350 degrees for 1 hour or until a tester inserted in the center comes out clean. Cut into squares and top with Brandy Sauce.

Yield: 8 servings

Brandy Sauce

1 cup (2 sticks) unsalted butter
1 cup packed brown sugar
1 cup heavy cream
1/4 cup brandy or bourbon

Combine the butter, brown sugar, cream and brandy in a saucepan and mix well. Bring to a boil over high heat. Cook until the butter melts, stirring constantly. Reduce the heat and simmer for 15 minutes, stirring frequently.

Yield: about 31/4 cups

A Party in the Kitchen

Menu

Chunky Guacamole

Blue Cheese Coleslaw

Braised Short Ribs

Creamy Mashed Potatoes

Cheddar Biscuits

Chocolate Cinnamon Pots de Crème

My three daughters, Lisa, Libby, and Sheri, are very good cooks. Lisa, in particular, enjoys entertaining family and friends. Her husband Paul enjoys grilling and is an excellent grill chef. I always suggest buffet service unless you are serving ten or less because it's much easier. The Chunky Guacamole is so healthy. You can find guacamole mix in the grocery store if you are saving time for other things or buy it already prepared. Don't forget the scoops. Blue Cheese Coleslaw is different and adds a lot to the menu. The Braised Short Ribs were the main course at Lisa's house recently on the night of Paul Jr.'s graduation from high school. How yummy are the Creamy Mashed Potatoes—they go really well with short ribs or just about anything! Don't forget to use White Lily flour for your biscuits. The Chocolate Cinnamon Pots de Crème are the "pièce de résistance" for dessert. Garnish with a dollop of whipped cream and a bit of grated chocolate.

Chunky Guacamole

3 ripe avocados
2 tablespoons minced onion
1 garlic clove, minced or
   pressed (about 1 teaspoon)
1 small jalapeño chile,
   minced
   (1 to 1¹/2 teaspoons)
¹/4 cup minced fresh
   cilantro leaves
¹/4 teaspoon salt
Juice of 1 lime
Salt to taste

Cut one of the avocados into halves and remove the pit. Scoop the avocado into a medium bowl. Add the onion, garlic, jalapeño chile, cilantro and ¹/4 teaspoon salt and mash with a fork until combined. Cut the remaining avocados into halves and remove the pits. Chop the avocados and add to the mashed avocado mixture. Sprinkle with the lime juice and mix lightly with a fork until combined but still chunky. Add salt to taste. Serve with tortilla chips or corn scoops. To make ahead, cover the guacamole with plastic wrap and press directly onto the surface to prevent browning. Chill for up to one day.

Yield: 8 servings

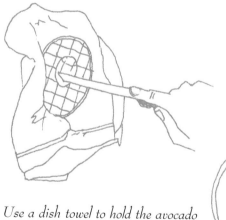

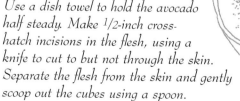

Use a dish towel to hold the avocado half steady. Make ¹/2-inch cross-hatch incisions in the flesh, using a knife to cut to but not through the skin. Separate the flesh from the skin and gently scoop out the cubes using a spoon.

Jalapeño Chiles

Seeded versus unseeded? Leaving the seeds in creates heat in a dish…if you desire a less spicy guacamole, wear latex gloves while seeding the jalapeño chiles to prevent burning your hands.

Blue Cheese Coleslaw

Use leftover coleslaw on a chicken or pork sandwich.

1/2 small head green cabbage
1/2 medium head red cabbage
4 large carrots
2 cups mayonnaise
2 tablespoons Dijon mustard
1 tablespoon whole grain
 mustard
2 tablespoons apple
 cider vinegar
1 teaspoon celery salt
1/2 teaspoon kosher salt
1/2 teaspoon freshly ground
 black pepper
1 1/2 cups (6 ounces)
 crumbled blue cheese or
 Roquefort cheese
1 cup chopped fresh
 flat-leaf parsley

Process the cabbage and carrots in a food processor fitted with the slicing knife or use the large side of a box grater or simply a sharp knife. Place in a large bowl, discarding any large pieces. Whisk the mayonnaise, Dijon mustard, whole grain mustard, vinegar, celery salt, kosher salt and pepper in a medium bowl. Pour enough of the dressing over the cabbage mixture to moisten and toss well. Add the blue cheese and parsley and toss well. Chill, covered with plastic wrap, for several hours to allow the flavors to meld. Serve cold or at room temperature.

Yield: 8 to 10 servings

Braised Short Ribs

6 beef short ribs
 (5 to 7 pounds)
1 tablespoon salt
2 teaspoons freshly
 ground pepper
3 tablespoons vegetable oil
3 carrots, cut into
 1-inch pieces
1 rib celery, chopped
1 onion, coarsely chopped
4 shallots, sliced
5 garlic cloves,
 cut into halves
3 tablespoons tomato paste
3 tablespoons all-purpose
 flour
4 cups full-bodied red wine,
 such as cabernet
 sauvignon
2 sprigs of rosemary
6 sprigs of thyme
6 cups veal stock

Sprinkle the short ribs with the salt and pepper. Heat the oil in a large Dutch oven over high heat. Add one-half of the short ribs. Cook in the hot oil for 3 minutes or until brown on all sides. Remove the short ribs and set aside. Repeat with the remaining short ribs. Reduce the heat to medium. Add the carrots, celery, onion, shallots and garlic to the pan drippings. Sauté for 5 minutes or until the onion is soft. Stir in the tomato paste. Add the flour and mix well. Add the wine, rosemary and thyme. Increase the heat to high. Cook until the liquid is reduced by one-third. Return the short ribs to the Dutch oven. Add the stock. Add enough water to cover the short ribs, if needed. Bake at 325 degrees for 4 hours. Serve over Creamy Mashed Potatoes (page 28).

Yield: 8 to 10 servings

If you have leftover short ribs, assemble lightly grilled flour tortillas with the shredded short ribs, chopped onion, tomato, cilantro, and a squirt of lime juice.

Creamy Mashed Potatoes

For a variation, use scrubbed unpeeled new potatoes—the red skins add great taste and texture.

5 pounds Yukon Gold
   potatoes, peeled and cut
   into 1-inch pieces
2 cups heavy cream or
   half-and-half
6 tablespoons unsalted
   butter, cut into pieces
2 teaspoons salt
1 teaspoon freshly ground
   pepper

Bring the potatoes and enough water to cover by 1 inch to a boil in a large saucepan over high heat. Reduce the heat to medium and simmer for 20 minutes or until the potatoes are tender. Heat the cream, butter, salt and pepper in a saucepan over medium heat for 5 minutes or until smooth, whisking constantly. Keep warm. Drain the potatoes and return to the saucepan. Add the cream mixture. Mash with a potato masher or with an electric mixer until creamy. Serve immediately.

Yield: 8 to 10 servings

White Lily Flour

White Lily flour is made from a softer, winter wheat. My mother used it exclusively. It makes very tender biscuits, and Southern cooks prefer it.

Cheddar Biscuits

2¹/₂ cups all-purpose flour
¹/₄ cup sugar
1 tablespoon baking powder
1 teaspoon kosher salt
6 tablespoons butter, chilled
   and cut into cubes
1 cup (4 ounces) shredded
   sharp Cheddar cheese
1 cup buttermilk
1 egg, beaten

Process the flour, sugar, baking powder and salt in a food processor until well mixed. Add the cold butter gradually and process until the consistency of cornmeal. Place in a medium bowl. Add the cheese and mix well. Combine the buttermilk and egg in a bowl and mix well. Add to the flour mixture and stir just until moistened. Drop by ¹/₄ cupfuls onto a lightly greased baking sheet. Bake at 450 degrees for 15 minutes or until the tops are golden brown.

Yield: 12 medium biscuits

Chocolate Cinnamon Pots de Crème

2 cups heavy cream
2 cups half-and-half
2/3 cup sugar
2/3 cup (4 ounces)
   bittersweet or semisweet
   chocolate chips
6 egg yolks
2 eggs
1/2 cup baking cocoa
1 teaspoon cinnamon
Pinch of salt
2 teaspoons vanilla extract
Whipped cream

Combine the cream, half-and-half, sugar and chocolate chips in a 2-quart microwave-safe glass measure. Microwave on High for 2 minutes. Whisk the mixture. Microwave for 2 minutes longer or until the steam rises and the chocolate chips are melted. Whisk the egg yolks, eggs, baking cocoa, cinnamon and salt together in a bowl. Add the warm chocolate mixture in a slow stream, whisking constantly. Stir in the vanilla. Strain into a glass measure with a pouring spout. Spoon off any foam. Divide among six 3-ounce pot de crème cups or oven-safe ramekins. Cover each cup tightly with a lid or foil. Arrange the cups in a baking pan, being careful not to let them touch each other or the sides of the pan. Add enough hot water to the pan to come halfway up the outside of the cups. Bake at 325 degrees for 35 minutes or until the custards are set but are still quivering like gelatin. Bake for 3 to 5 minutes longer if needed. Remove from the water bath and cool for 30 minutes at room temperature. Chill for 8 to 10 hours. Garnish with whipped cream. This recipe may be doubled.

Yield: 6 servings

I gave my favorite aunts pots de crème cups and now I have them to serve these delicious desserts in. You can bake in them and they are lovely. You can vary the flavor of this recipe from chocolate to pumpkin by leaving out chocolate and adding 1 cup canned pumpkin to the egg yolk mixture. These elegant desserts are easy to make ahead and chill. Custard cups can be used if pot de crème cups are not available.

A Casual Company Supper

Menu

Chutney Cheese

Tarragon Deviled Eggs

Shrimp and Grits with Applewood Bacon

Pecan Beet Salad

Tarragon Deviled Eggs

Pecan-Beet Salad

Scoop-and-Bake Dinner Rolls

Quick Apple Tart or Chocolate Cobbler

Entertaining is merely sharing good food and drink with family and friends. This menu is easy to assemble, and the Shrimp and Grits are "to die for." Be sure to make out your grocery list and organization timetable early in the week. Locate a colorful quilt for the food table, festive napkins, and a bunch of fresh flowers, veggies, or fresh fruit in a basket for the centerpiece. The Chutney Cheese is a breeze to prepare—it can be prepared early and refrigerated. The Shrimp and Grits are one of my favorite recipes and can be prepared several hours ahead and reheated. If you don't care for beets, substitute a salad from the salad section—but the beets can be roasted the day before. Tarragon Deviled Eggs add so much to this menu. Like the French, I adore tarragon. Add some to your chicken salad when you get the urge to make chicken salad. The Scoop-and-Bake Rolls are easy. Take your pick of the desserts. Both are divine and can be made ahead. Most of all, enjoy your friends. Relax.

Chutney Cheese

16 ounces cream cheese,
softened
1 (8-ounce) jar Major Grey's
chutney
1/2 cup chopped green
onions (about 1 bunch)
1/2 cup coarsely chopped dry
roasted peanuts
1/2 cup flaked coconut

Spread the cream cheese evenly on a small serving plate. Pour the chutney over the cream cheese. Layer the green onions, peanuts and coconut over the chutney. Serve immediately or chill for up to 1 hour. Serve with crackers.

Yield: 10 to 12 servings

Tarragon Deviled Eggs

You may stuff a hard-cooked egg with everything from crab meat and chipotle seasoning to pimento cheese and bacon. The addition of tarragon adds a special taste to these deviled eggs. They are great for a cocktail party, too.

6 hard-cooked eggs
1/4 cup mayonnaise
2 teaspoons Dijon mustard
2 teaspoons sugar
1/2 teaspoon fresh tarragon
Salt and pepper to taste
Flat-leaf parsley for garnish

Cut the hard-cooked eggs into halves crosswise or lengthwise as desired. Remove the yolks and place in a sealable plastic bag. Add the mayonnaise, mustard, sugar, tarragon, salt and pepper and seal the bag. Mash the bag to mix the ingredients. Cut a corner from the bag and pipe into the egg whites. Garnish each with a piece of parsley. Chill, covered, until serving time.

Yield: 12 deviled eggs

Achieve a lighter taste and texture by substituting Neufchâtel cheese for cream cheese in the Chutney Cheese—it contains one-third less fat.

Shrimp and Cheese Grits with Applewood Bacon

*My sweet friend Joan Barksdale does another rendition of
this yummy dish, which is my favorite casual meal.*

*Originally termed
"Breakfast Shrimp," this
began as a breakfast dish
for coastal fishermen
during the shrimp season
(May through December)
in Charleston and the rest
of South Carolina's Low
Country. It has become
a lunch and dinner favorite
in gourmet restaurants
across the South.*

8 slices applewood-smoked
  bacon, chopped
1 tablespoon minced garlic
1 tablespoon minced shallots
3 tablespoons butter
2 splashes of white wine
1 pound peeled and deveined
  jumbo shrimp
1 portabella mushroom cap,
  domestic white mushroom
  cap or shiitake mushroom
  cap, sliced
1/4 cup chopped scallions
2 cups heavy cream
Salt and pepper to taste
Hot pepper sauce to taste
Cheese Grits (below)

Cook the bacon in a large skillet over medium heat for 3 minutes. Add the garlic and shallots. Sauté until the shallots are tender. Add the butter and white wine. Cook until the butter begins to melt. Add the shrimp. Sauté until the shrimp begins to turn pink. Turn the shrimp and add the mushroom and scallions. Sauté for 2 minutes or until the shrimp turns pink. Remove the shrimp and set aside. Add the cream to the mushroom mixture. Simmer until the mixture is reduced by one-third, stirring constantly. Add salt, pepper and hot sauce. Return the shrimp to the skillet and mix well. Serve over Cheese Grits.

Yield: 8 servings

Cheese Grits

4 cups milk
1 cup half-and-half
1/2 cup (1 stick) unsalted
  butter
1 1/2 cups uncooked
  stone ground or
  quick cooking grits
1 egg, lightly beaten
Salt and white pepper
  to taste
2 cups (8 ounces) shredded
  Swiss cheese or asiago
  cheese

Bring the milk, half-and-half and butter to a boil in a heavy saucepan over medium heat, stirring frequently. Add the grits and mix well. Reduce the heat and simmer until creamy and thickened, stirring occasionally. Remove from the heat. Add a small amount of the hot mixture to the egg. Add the egg to the hot mixture. Stir in salt and white pepper. Add the cheese and mix well.

Yield: 8 servings

Pecan-Beet Salad

There are many varieties of beets: candy cane, golden, and white.
Pickling is easy—just slice roasted beets and add sugar and apple cider
vinegar. Marinate for several hours and drain.

6 (6-ounce) golden beets
1 cup pecan halves
3/4 cup rice wine vinegar
1 large shallot, minced
2 tablespoons light
    brown sugar
1/2 teaspoon salt
1/2 teaspoon freshly
    ground pepper
1/2 teaspoon vanilla extract
1/4 cup canola oil
1 (5-ounce) package gourmet
    mixed salad greens, rinsed
    and drained
1 cup (4 ounces) crumbled
    Gorgonzola cheese

Trim the beet stems to 1 inch. Gently wash
the beets. Wrap each beet in foil and place
on a jelly-roll pan. Bake at 400 degrees for
1 hour or until tender. Remove to a wire rack.
Let stand, wrapped in foil, for 30 minutes or
until cool. Reduce the oven temperature to
350 degrees. Spread the pecans in a single
layer in a jelly-roll pan. Bake for 5 to 7 minutes
or until lightly toasted and fragrant. Let cool
on a wire rack for 15 minutes. Whisk the
vinegar, shallot, brown sugar, salt, pepper and
vanilla in a small bowl until well mixed. Add
the oil in a slow steady stream, whisking
constantly. Peel the roasted beets and remove
the stem ends. Cut the beets into 1/2-inch
wedges and place in a bowl. Add 1/3 cup of the
vinaigrette and toss gently to coat. Arrange
the salad greens on a serving platter. Add
the beet mixture, cheese and toasted pecans
and toss to mix. Serve with the remaining
vinaigrette. If you are in a hurry, you may
use thoroughly drained canned beets.

Yield: 8 servings

Scoop-and-Bake Dinner Rolls

Use an ice cream scoop for uniform rolls.

2¹/4 cups all-purpose flour

¹/4 cup sugar

1 teaspoon salt

1 envelope fast-rising yeast
    or instant yeast
    (2¹/4 teaspoons)

1 cup water, heated to
    110 degrees

6 tablespoons unsalted
    butter, softened

1 egg

Adjust the oven rack to the center position. Preheat the oven to 200 degrees. Maintain the oven temperature for 10 minutes and then turn off the oven. Whisk 1¹/4 cups of the flour, the sugar, salt and yeast together in a large bowl. Add the water, butter and egg and whisk for 2 minutes or until smooth. Add the remaining 1 cup flour and mix with a rubber spatula just until combined. Cover the bowl with greased plastic wrap. Place in the warm oven. Let rise for 30 minutes or until the dough is doubled in bulk. Remove from the oven and punch the dough down. Scoop the dough evenly into greased muffin cups. Cover with greased plastic wrap. Let rise at room temperature for 15 minutes or until the dough nearly reaches the rims of the muffin cups. Remove the plastic wrap. Bake at 375 degrees for 14 to 18 minutes or until golden. The rolls can be stored in an airtight container at room temperature for three days.

Yield: 1 dozen rolls

Quick Apple Tart

Make a gourmet ice cream to accompany the tart by stirring apple pie spice mix into softened, store-bought vanilla ice cream. Refreeze until serving time.

1 sheet frozen puff pastry, thawed
3 Golden Delicious apples, peeled and thinly sliced
2 tablespoons unsalted butter, melted
3 tablespoons cinnamon-sugar
1/4 cup apricot jam, melted

Unfold the pastry on a baking sheet lined with baking parchment. Pierce a 1/2-inch border around the edge of the pastry with the tines of a fork. Continue to pierce the entire center. Arrange the apples in four overlapping rows on top of the pastry, leaving the border clear. Brush the apples with the melted butter. Sprinkle with the cinnamon-sugar. Bake at 400 degrees for 30 minutes. Brush the melted jam over the apples. Bake for 8 minutes or until golden brown. Serve warm or at room temperature.

Yield: 6 servings

Chocolate Cobbler

1 cup (2 sticks) butter or margarine
11/4 cups sugar
11/2 cups self-rising flour
1 teaspoon vanilla extract
3/4 cup milk
1 cup sugar
6 tablespoons baking cocoa
2 cups boiling water

Place the butter in a 9×13-inch glass baking dish. Bake at 350 degrees until the butter melts. Maintain the oven temperature. Mix 11/4 cups sugar, the flour, vanilla and milk in a bowl. Pour over the melted butter. Do not stir. Mix 1 cup sugar and the baking cocoa together in a bowl. Sprinkle over the batter. Do not stir. Pour the boiling water over the top. Do not stir. Bake for 30 to 45 minutes or until golden brown.

Yield: 6 to 8 servings

Garnish chocolate desserts with whipped cream and chocolate curls. Place a large chocolate bar in the freezer for 10 to 20 minutes, and then scrape a vegetable peeler along the side of the bar.

A Small Plate
Appetizer Buffet

Menu

Cheese and Fruit Board

Brat Bites with Plum Sauce

Bette Davis Eyes

All-American Sliders

Smoked Salmon Spread

Caramelized Pear and Gruyère Torta

Hot Spinach Bacon Dip

Brownies with Chocolate Ganache Glaze

Coconut Truffles

Small bites, big fun—commonly known as Tapas (no, not topless). Invite your friends over for a laid-back get-together and offer tasty appetizers. Guests will want to sample all of these taste bud-tempting dishes. Position a large cheese tray, covered in fig leaves if seasonal, at one end of the table with goat cheese, blue cheese, Brie, and Havarti, surrounded by clumps of artfully arranged white and red seedless grapes. Walnuts and marcona almonds scattered among the cheeses dress up the cheese board. Crostini and small bowls of marmalade and chutney make it easy to build your own creations. The Brat Bites are delicious with Plum Sauce. The sauce can be made the day before and the brats grilled earlier in the day of the get-together. "Bette Davis Eyes" were a discovery of Nicole Shelton during a book-signing trip. They are such an interesting conversation sensation. The Smoked Salmon Spread and the Caramelized Pear and Gruyère Torta can be made the day before and refrigerated. The Hot Spinach Bacon Dip also can be prepared in advance and tucked into the refrigerator along with the Coconut Truffles and brownies. Fabulous pick-up foods enjoyed with good friends make for a great party you'll want to host again. Use greenery and flowers plus votive candles for the table or refer to decorating ideas on page 180. Be sure you have colorful cocktail napkins and plenty of ice on hand for drinks and water.

Brat Bites with Plum Sauce

My friend, Eydie Swanson, serves her brats with sautéed onions and green and red bell peppers plus a bit of mustard.

2 tablespoons fresh
ginger, minced
1/4 teaspoon Chinese five-
spice powder
1/4 teaspoon red pepper
flakes
2 teaspoons vegetable oil
1/2 cup plum jam
2 tablespoons rice vinegar
1 tablespoon soy sauce
1/4 teaspoon toasted
sesame oil
4 bratwursts, precooked
12 cocktail buns
6 scallions, cut into
3-inch lengths
1 tablespoon sesame seeds,
toasted
Hot mustard

Sauté the ginger, five-spice powder and pepper flakes in the vegetable oil in a small saucepan over medium heat. Cook for 2 minutes or until the ginger softens, stirring constantly. Stir in the jam, vinegar and soy sauce. Simmer for 5 minutes or until the sauce thickens. Remove from the heat. Whisk in the sesame oil. Place the bratwurst on a grill rack. Grill for 5 to 6 minutes or until brown and heated through. Cut the bratwurst crosswise into thirds. Toss with the plum sauce in a bowl. To assemble, cut a slit in the top of each cocktail bun. Tuck one or two scallion pieces and a piece of bratwurst inside each bun. Drizzle with some of the plum sauce. Sprinkle with the sesame seeds. Top with a small dollop of mustard.

Yield: 12 bites

Bette Davis Eyes

1/4 cup whipping cream
16 ounces goat cheese, at
room temperature
1 1/2 pounds globe grapes
(dark seedless)
2 cups finely chopped
pistachios

Mix the cream and goat cheese together in a bowl. Wrap some of the goat cheese mixture around each grape to cover. Roll in the pistachios to coat. Place in a container. Chill, covered, until serving time. To serve, cut each grape into halves. Arrange on a platter lined with lettuce leaves.

Yield: 25 cocktail servings

Goat cheese is wrapped around grapes for the Bette Davis Eyes. I often tell my classes that goat cheese tastes like a goat smells. I am an authority, as we had a goat when the kids were growing up. I could write a whole book about Joshua Q. Freckle, the goat.

All-American Sliders

1 pound ground sirloin
1 tablespoon Worcestershire
   sauce
1 tablespoon steak sauce
1/2 teaspoon garlic powder
1/2 teaspoon onion powder
6 slider buns or mini
   sandwich rolls
6 slices sharp Cheddar cheese
6 pieces green leaf lettuce
Ketchup
Tangy Mayo (at left)
Pickles and cherry tomatoes
   for garnish

Combine the ground sirloin, Worcestershire sauce, steak sauce, garlic powder and onion powder in a bowl and mix well. Shape into six small patties. Place on a grill rack. Grill, covered with the grill lid, over medium-high heat (350 to 400 degrees) for 5 to 6 minutes or until cooked through. Serve on the buns with the cheese, lettuce, ketchup and Tangy Mayo. Garnish with pickles and cherry tomatoes.

Yield: 6 small burgers

Tangy Mayo

3/4 cup mayonnaise
1 tablespoon Dijon
   mustard
1 tablespoon steak sauce

Whisk the mayonnaise, mustard and steak sauce together in a small bowl. Spoon into an airtight container. Store in the refrigerator for up to one week.

Yield: about 1 cup

Smoked Salmon Spread

Easy to make and easy to eat.

12 ounces cream cheese,
   softened
1/3 cup sour cream
1 tablespoon fresh
   lemon juice
6 dashes of Tabasco sauce
White and green portions of
   3 scallions, sliced
3 tablespoons capers
8 ounces smoked salmon,
   coarsely chopped
3 tablespoons chopped fresh
   dill weed
Freshly ground pepper
   to taste
Dill weed for garnish
Crostini or assorted crackers

Purée the cream cheese, sour cream, lemon juice and Tabasco sauce in a food processor. Add the scallions, capers, salmon, 3 tablespoons dill weed and pepper and pulse just until blended. Spoon into a small serving bowl. Garnish with dill weed. Serve with crostini.

Yield: 10 to 12 servings

Caramelized Pear and Gruyère Torta

What a great combination!

2 tablespoons butter
1/2 cup sugar
4 large green Anjou
    pears, chopped
32 ounces Neufchâtel cheese
    or cream cheese, softened
2 cups (8 ounces) shredded
    Gruyère cheese or
    Swiss cheese
1 cup chopped pistachios

Melt the butter in a large saucepan over medium-high heat. Stir in the sugar and pears until well mixed. Cook for 12 to 15 minutes or until the liquid thickens and the pears begin to caramelize. Remove from the heat and set aside to cool completely. Beat the Neufchâtel cheese and Gruyère cheese at medium speed in a medium mixing bowl until well combined. Line an 8-inch baking pan with plastic wrap. Spread one-half of the cheese mixture in the bottom of the prepared pan. Spread one-half of the pear mixture over the cheese mixture. Top with the remaining cheese mixture. Chill for 1 hour. Invert the torta onto a serving dish and remove the pan. Remove the plastic wrap carefully. Cover the side of the torta with the pistachios. Top with the remaining pear mixture. Chill, covered, until serving time. Serve with crackers.

Yield: 10 to 12 servings

Hot Spinach Bacon Dip

Who does not like spinach dip?

1 pound sliced bacon
1 (10-ounce) package frozen
  chopped spinach, thawed
  and well drained
8 ounces cream cheese,
  softened
1 cup sour cream
1 (10-ounce) can extra-hot
  tomatoes with green
  chiles, drained
1 cup (4 ounces) shredded
  Cheddar cheese
1 cup (4 ounces) shredded
  Parmesan cheese
1/2 teaspoon fresh
  minced garlic
4 to 5 green onions, chopped
Chips

Brown the bacon in a large skillet over medium heat. Remove the bacon to paper towels to drain. Crumble the bacon and set aside. Cook the spinach, cream cheese and sour cream in a medium saucepan over medium heat until bubbly, stirring frequently. Add the tomatoes with green chiles, Cheddar cheese and Parmesan cheese. Cook until the cheese is melted, stirring frequently. Stir in the garlic, green onions and bacon. Keep warm until serving time. Serve warm with chips.

Yield: 25 servings

Brownies with Chocolate Ganache Glaze

These are the best you've eaten and so easy.

4 ounces unsweetened
  chocolate
1/2 cup (1 stick) butter
1/2 cup (1 stick) margarine
2 cups sugar
4 eggs, beaten
1 cup all-purpose flour
1/2 teaspoon salt
Chocolate Ganache Glaze
  (at right)

Combine the chocolate, butter and margarine in a 2-quart microwave-safe dish. Microwave on High at 30-second intervals until melted and smooth, stirring after each interval. Combine the sugar and eggs in a bowl and mix well. Stir in the chocolate mixture, flour and salt. Spoon into a 9×12-inch baking pan coated with nonstick cooking spray. Bake at 350 degrees for 20 minutes. Let stand until cool. Spread with the Chocolate Ganache Glaze. Cut into squares.

Yield: 2 dozen

Chocolate Ganache Glaze

2 cups (12 ounces)
  chocolate chips
1 cup whipping cream

Place the chocolate chips in a 2-quart microwave-safe glass measure. Microwave on Medium for 2 minutes. Whisk and microwave on Medium for 2 more minutes. Whisk in the whipping cream until smooth.

Yield: about 3 cups

Coconut Truffles

Add an elegant touch to any party.

2 cups shredded coconut
1/4 cup (1/2 stick) butter
1/3 cup whipping cream
7 ounces semisweet
  chocolate
1 egg yolk
1 teaspoon vanilla extract

Spread the coconut on a baking sheet. Bake at 250 degrees for 8 minutes or until toasted, stirring frequently. Place the butter, whipping cream and chocolate in a 2-quart microwave-safe glass measure. Microwave on Medium for 2 minutes. Whisk the mixture. Microwave for 2 minutes longer and whisk again. Continue until the mixture is smooth. Whisk a small amount of the hot mixture into the egg yolk. Whisk the egg yolk quickly into the hot mixture. Stir in the vanilla. Chill until firm. Shape into 1-inch balls and roll in the toasted coconut to coat. Store in the refrigerator. Place in miniature silver or gold foil candy cups to serve.

Yield: about 30 servings

A French Dinner
"Celebrating Julia"

Menu

Ham and Gruyère Cheese Puffs

Tapenade

Green Salad with Tarragon and Mint

Supremes de Volaille à la Milanaise (Parmesan Chicken Breasts)

Épinard à la Crème (Creamed Spinach)

Pear Tarte Tatin

During the last ten years, I have had the fabulous experience of spending days in France, Provence to be exact, at La Pitchoune, the château previously owned by Julia Child and now owned by Kathy Alex, a California native. It is here that Julia and Simone Beck wrote *Mastering the Art of French Cooking*. Each time we are there, we visit our dear friend Nall Hollis, in Vence, a very famous artist from Arab, Alabama. He lives in Point Clear, Alabama, for six months of the year and Vence, France, for six months. Nall studied under Salvador Dali, who prophesied that when he died, Nall would be the most famous artist in Europe, which he is.

Kathy Alex teaches French cooking classes, introduces you to French markets, cheese caves, restaurants, etc., in the Grasse area near Valbonne. Last summer we rented Julia's small, unassuming château and were accompanied by our three girls, Libby Patrick, Sheri Hofherr, and Lisa Wallace. We also had with us three grandchildren: Alex Patrick and Finlay and Brandon Hofherr. What a fabulous trip!

A French proverb says, "A good meal ought to begin with hunger." Here's hoping your guests are hungry when you serve them this dinner. The Ham and Gruyère Cheese Puffs can be prepared and baked early the day of the event and rewarmed before serving. The salad greens and herbs can be washed, dried, and stored in sealable plastic bags (What did we ever do without them?) The dressing, which should be refrigerated, also can be made the day before. Whisk again before mixing with the greens. The chicken breasts may be breaded and placed in the refrigerator the day before. Sauté late in the day and keep warm until you serve with the wine sauce. The spinach needs to be done an hour before serving. Pear Tarte Tatin is a "work of art" but not difficult. The tart can be prepared ahead but baked as your guests sit down to dinner. Remember the French are insulted if you do not dine slowly and savor each bite. Serve buffet style if you have more than eight to ten guests.

Ham and Gruyère Cheese Puffs

These are so good. We were, of course, at La Pitchoune preparing these in Julia's very small former kitchen. You can almost feel her presence when you are there.

1 egg, beaten
1 tablespoon water
1 sheet puff pastry
Finely shredded
   Gruyère cheese
3-inch strips of ham

Beat the egg with the water in a small bowl. Roll the puff pastry 1/4 inch thick on a lightly floured surface. Cut into long 3-inch strips. Sprinkle with the cheese and press into the pastry. Layer the ham over the cheese. Fold the pastry lengthwise into thirds, pressing to seal. Cut crosswise into 1-inch strips. Brush with the egg wash to seal. Place seam side down on a baking sheet. Bake at 450 degrees for 15 minutes or until brown.

Yield: 8 servings

Tapenade

As an appetizer before dinner, the French generally serve a tapenade or radishes dipped in salt.

12 ounces pitted black
   olives
2 tablespoons capers
4 ounces anchovy
   fillets, drained

Process the olives, capers and anchovy fillets in a food processor to form a thick paste. Spoon into a container. Store, covered, in the refrigerator for up to three weeks. Serve with assorted crackers or thin slices of French bread or bâtarde.

Yield: about 2 cups

Green Salad with Tarragon and Mint

The French love tarragon, and fresh mint has been added to this recipe.
This salad goes well with almost any menu.

It was so much fun
shopping in the various
French markets. The
vegetables, meats, fish,
terrines, and pastries are
all beautifully fresh.
I especially loved the
market in Cannes, France.
Throughout the town are
small, very special pastry
shops. The plane landed in
Paris, and we spent two
days there before going to
Valbonne. In Paris, I
always make a trip to
Fauchon's, which carries
the finest foods in the
world. It is located on
Madeleine Square.
Gorgeous pastries are
displayed in the windows.

2 tablespoons balsamic
    vinegar or white
    wine vinegar
2 tablespoons fresh
    lemon juice
6 tablespoons extra-virgin
    olive oil
6 tablespoons honey
18 cups mixed baby greens
1/2 cup fresh tarragon
1 cup fresh mint
Coarse salt and freshly
    ground pepper to taste

Whisk the vinegar and lemon juice together in a large bowl. Add the olive oil in a slow steady stream, whisking constantly until emulsified. Whisk in the honey. Add the greens, tarragon, mint, salt and pepper and toss to coat.

Yield: 10 servings

Julia's kitchen at La Pitchoune just as she left it.

Suprêmes de Volaille à la Milanaise (Chicken Breasts Rolled in Parmesan and Fresh Bread Crumbs)

2 cups all-purpose flour

2 eggs

1/2 teaspoon salt

2 teaspoons olive oil

1 cup (4 ounces) freshly
    grated Parmesan cheese

1 cup fresh fine white
    bread crumbs

8 suprêmes (boned chicken
    breasts from four fryers)

1/2 teaspoon salt

Big pinch of pepper

Clarified butter for sautéing

1 tablespoon minced shallots
    or green onions

1/4 cup port, madeira,
    marsala or any white wine

2/3 cup brown stock or
    canned beef bouillon

2 tablespoons minced parsley

Spread the flour in an 8-inch pie plate. Beat the eggs, 1/2 teaspoon salt and the olive oil in an 8-inch soup plate. Whisk the Parmesan cheese and bread crumbs together in an 8-inch bowl. Sprinkle the chicken with 1/2 teaspoon salt and pepper. Roll the chicken breasts one at a time in the flour to coat and shake off the excess. Dip in the beaten egg mixture and roll in the bread crumb mixture, patting in place with the flat side of a knife. Place the chicken breasts in a single layer on waxed paper and let stand for 10 to 15 minutes or chill for several hours to allow the cheese and bread crumbs to set. Sauté the chicken breasts in clarified butter in a skillet until cooked through. Remove to a serving dish and keep warm. Sauté the shallots in the pan drippings in the skillet. Add the wine and stock. Boil rapidly over high heat until the liquid is slightly syrupy. Pour over the chicken. Sprinkle with the parsley and serve.

Yield: 8 servings

You can make your own fresh bread crumbs by pulsing leftover bread in your food processor fitted with the metal blade. Dry bread makes better crumbs. Any leftover crumbs may be stored in a sealable freezer bag in the freezer for future use.

Épinard à la Crème
(Spinach Braised in Cream)

Julia's quote: "If you can't use butter, use cream." Rich, creamy, and yummy, creamed spinach is one of my favorites. Use a bit of freshly grated nutmeg. To make it a bit lighter, you may use brown stock or canned beef bouillon.

9 cups cooked chopped
   spinach
3 tablespoons butter,
   softened
Salt and pepper to taste
4 1/2 tablespoons flour, sifted
2 to 3 cups whipping cream
3 tablespoons butter,
   softened

Place the spinach in a heavy enameled saucepan. Add 3 tablespoons butter, salt and pepper. Cook over medium heat until the liquid has evaporated. Sprinkle with the flour. Cook for 2 minutes, whisking constantly. Remove from the heat. Stir in 2 cups of the cream gradually. Bring to a simmer. Simmer, covered, for 15 minutes, stirring frequently to prevent the spinach from sticking to the bottom of the saucepan and adding the remaining cream, if needed. Adjust the seasonings to taste. Remove from the heat. Fold in 3 tablespoons butter. Spoon into a serving dish. If the spinach is not served immediately, top with 1 tablespoon cream and set aside uncovered. Reheat when needed.

Yield: 8 to 10 servings

Pear Tarte Tatin

This does take a bit of time but is lovely and so French.

6 ripe unblemished Comice
    or Bartlett pears
Juice of 2 lemons
1 cup sugar
1/4 cup water
1/4 teaspoon lemon juice
1/4 cup (1/2 stick) unsalted
    butter, cut into
    small pieces
1 disk Pâte Brisée (below)

Peel the pears and cut into halves. Sprinkle with the juice of 2 lemons to prevent browning. Mix the sugar, water and 1/4 teaspoon lemon juice in an 11-inch heavy ovenproof skillet. Bring to a boil. Reduce the heat and cook until the sugar syrup is amber in color. Remove immediately from the heat. Stir in the butter. Arrange the pear halves cut side up in a neat overlapping pattern in the caramelized sugar. Cook over low heat for 10 minutes or until the sugar syrup thickens and is reduced by one-half. Remove from the heat to cool. Roll the pastry 1/8 inch thick on a lightly floured surface. Place over the pear halves and trim the edge. Bake at 375 degrees for 20 minutes or until the pastry is golden brown. Remove from the oven. Let cool for 10 to 15 minutes. Loosen the pastry from the side of the skillet using a sharp knife. Place a serving platter over the skillet and quickly invert to release the tarte Tatin onto the serving platter. Serve immediately.

Yield: 8 servings

Pâte Brisée (Perfect Pastry)

2 cups all-purpose flour
1/2 teaspoon salt
3/4 cup (1 1/2 sticks) unsalted
    butter, chilled and cut
    into pieces
1/4 cup ice water

Process the flour and salt in a food processor for several seconds. Add the butter and process until crumbly. Add the ice water gradually, processing just until blended. Divide the dough into two equal portions. Shape each portion into a disk. Wrap each disk in plastic wrap and chill in the refrigerator.

Yield: 2 pastries

A few years ago, I was attending a cooking class in Paris with Jackie Guice and my daughter Libby. We had worked in class making our tarte Tatin so beautiful, artfully layering the pear slices, and we baked it. After the class, we all went to enjoy a lunch of the things we had prepared. We were ready for dessert, when we heard a crash in the kitchen. The assistant had dropped our Pear Tarte Tatin! Oh dear, obviously it was not so beautiful, but it was excellent in taste.

A Taste of Tuscany:
An Italian Dinner

Menu

Prosecco Royale

Antipasto Platter

Avocado-Tomato Salad

Roast Pork with Rosemary and Thyme with a Mustard Wine Sauce

Polenta with Mascarpone Cheese

Cabbage Braised with White Wine

Panna Cotta with Balsamic Berries

Focaccia or Italian Herb Breadsticks

A few years ago we were traveling in Italy with our dear friends, Mackie and Jim Gibb Johnson, it was such a special time. Jim Gibb and Bill actually grew up together in Knoxville, were in Scouts together, and eventually both became doctors. This particular trip with the Johnsons began in Rome, then on to Florence, San Gimignano, Pisa, and Montepulciano. While in Montepulciano, Mackie and I were very fortunate to be able to attend cooking classes conducted by Pamela Sheldon Johns, an American native who has lived in Italy many years and has written several books about the artisans of Italy. We, of course, toured many museums in all the cities, but I snuck away in Florence for a cooking class in Artimino at Ristorante "Da Delfido." Among other things, we prepared Rabbit Stew, using many herbs from the owner-chef's garden. While there we were priviledged to taste 100-year-old balsamic vinegar (so thick, and sweet, and delicious) on fresh fruit. This is my idea of a perfect day—learning customs of other cultures. Italians are very friendly and hospitable.

The Roast Pork can be prepared or stuffed the day before roasting and refrigerated. Remove from the refrigerator an hour or so before cooking. It could be cooked late in the afternoon the day of dinner. The Antipasto Platter, the Focaccia Bread, and the Panna Cotta can be prepared the day before your event as well. Your Tomato-Avocado Salad and the Braised Cabbage can be done an hour or so before guests arrive. I always suggest a buffet service if you are having more than eight or ten guests. Set your table the day before and use a pretty bowl filled with fruit or refer to the table decorating ideas on page 180. If you like this menu, Tuscany is truly a place you would enjoy visiting.

Prosecco Royale

1/2 cup sugar
1/2 cup water
1 cup fresh cranberries
1 (750-milliliter) bottle
   prosecco, chilled

Chill six Champagne flutes. Heat the sugar and water in a small saucepan over low heat for 5 minutes or until the sugar dissolves, stirring constantly. Add the cranberries. Bring to a boil. Reduce the heat and simmer for 2 minutes. Strain the syrup into a sealable container and place the cranberries in a separate container. Chill until serving time. To serve, place a few of the cranberries in each flute and top each with 1 tablespoon of the cranberry syrup. Fill each flute with the prosecco. You may serve prosecco as it comes from the bottle, as this is what is popular in Italy.

Yield: 6 drinks

Avocado-Tomato Salad

2 ripe avocados, cut into
   halves and sliced
2 ripe plum tomatoes, sliced
2 tablespoons olive oil
2 tablespoons fresh
   lemon juice
1 tablespoon fresh oregano
   leaves, or 1/4 teaspoon
   dried oregano
1/4 teaspoon salt
1/8 teaspoon pepper

Toss the avocados and tomatoes together gently in a serving bowl. Combine the olive oil, lemon juice, oregano, salt and pepper in a small cup and mix well. Drizzle over the avocado mixture. Adjust the salt and pepper to taste.

Yield: 6 servings

Antipasto Platter

An antipasto platter served before the meal literally means "before the pasta." It is served with various Italian wines.

Marinated olives
Sliced smoked meats
Assortment of cheeses
Grapes for garnish

Assemble marinated olives, smoked meats, and an assortment of cheeses on a serving platter. Garnish with grapes.

Yield: a variable amount

Roast Pork with Rosemary and Thyme

1 (4- to 5-pound) boneless
   pork loin
3 garlic cloves, minced
2 tablespoons chopped fresh
   rosemary
Salt and freshly ground
   pepper to taste
1/4 cup extra-virgin olive oil
4 sprigs of fresh rosemary
Mustard Wine Sauce (below)

Cut the pork down the side and ends and open as for a book. Mix the garlic, chopped rosemary, salt and pepper with one-half of the olive oil in a cup. Spread over the pork. Place the rosemary sprigs over the top. Tie the pork back together with kitchen string. Rub with the remaining olive oil. Place in a baking pan. Bake at 350 degrees for 1 hour or until the pork is cooked through. Discard the string. Cut into slices and serve with Mustard Wine Sauce.

Yield: 8 to 10 servings

Mustard Wine Sauce

1 cup mayonnaise
1 cup sour cream
3 tablespoons grainy mustard
1/4 cup white wine
1/4 cup minced fresh parsley

Combine the mayonnaise, sour cream, mustard, wine and parsley in a bowl and mix well. Store in an airtight container until serving time.

Yield: about 2 1/2 cups

Rosemary is so wonderful with pork. Rosemary fronds or skewers may be used for grilling anything you might use a skewer for—vegetables, shrimp, chunks of pork tenderloin, etc. It is also wonderful as an aromatic and can serve as an antioxidant. I gather a bouquet of it every few days for my kitchen.

Polenta with Mascarpone Cheese

1/4 cup olive oil
1 cup chopped onion
9 cups chicken stock
3 cups polenta or plain
   yellow cornmeal
1/2 cup (2 ounces) grated
   Parmigiano-Reggiano
   cheese
8 ounces mascarpone cheese
Salt and freshly ground
   pepper to taste

Heat the olive oil in a large sauté pan over medium-high heat. Add the onion and sauté for 3 to 4 minutes or until golden brown. Add the stock. Bring to a boil. Whisk in the polenta gradually. Cook for 25 to 30 minutes or until the polenta pulls away from the side of the pan, whisking constantly. Stir in the Parmigiano-Reggiano cheese, mascarpone cheese, salt and pepper. Spoon into a serving dish and serve immediately.

Yield: 8 servings

Cabbage Braised in White Wine

Always use wine for cooking that you would drink. It really makes a difference.

3 pounds savoy cabbage
3 tablespoons extra-virgin
   olive oil
4 ounces pancetta or
   bacon, chopped
Salt and freshly ground
   pepper to taste
3/4 cup dry white wine

Remove the hard core from the cabbage. Cut the cabbage leaves into narrow strips. Heat the olive oil in a heavy saucepan over medium heat. Add the pancetta. Fry for 5 minutes or until transparent. Add the cabbage and mix well. Cook gently for a few minutes to blend the flavors. Sprinkle with salt and pepper. Add the wine. Cook, covered, over low heat for 20 minutes or until the cabbage is very tender, checking occasionally and adding a couple of tablespoons of water if needed. Arrange the cabbage on a serving platter and serve hot.

Yield: 8 servings

Chill leftover polenta. Spread in a greased rimmed baking sheet. Cut into triangles or squares and lightly sprinkle with flour. Fry in a mixture of butter and olive oil in a skillet until golden brown. These are delicious under vegetables or any meat for another meal.

Focaccia

1 envelope dry yeast
3/4 cup lukewarm water
2 cups all-purpose flour
1/2 teaspoon salt
1/4 cup olive oil
Sliced or quartered green
    and black olives
Chopped fresh herbs,
    especially rosemary
Thinly sliced onions
Shaved prosciutto or ham
Sliced mushrooms
Pine nuts (optional)

Dissolve the yeast in the lukewarm water in a bowl and mix well. Let stand for 5 minutes. Process the flour and salt in a food processor fitted with a dough blade or a metal blade. Add the yeast mixture and 3 tablespoons of the olive oil. Process to form a soft dough. Knead on a lightly floured surface for 2 minutes or until smooth and elastic, adding additional flour as needed to form an easily handled dough. Place in a greased bowl, turning to coat the surface. Let rise, covered with plastic wrap, in a warm place for 1 hour or until doubled in bulk. Punch the dough down. Let rest for 5 minutes. Pat into a 10-inch circle on a greased baking pan or into a 9×13-inch rectangle on a baking sheet. Press your fingers into the dough to make deep indentions. Do not press all the way through the dough. Brush with the remaining 1 tablespoon olive oil. Sprinkle with the olives, herbs, onions, prosciutto and mushrooms. Let rise, covered, for 15 minutes. Bake at 425 degrees for 20 to 25 minutes or until golden brown. Let cool in the pan on a wire rack. Sprinkle with pine nuts just before serving.

Yield: 8 to 10 servings

Use leftover focaccia for tasty little finger sandwiches. Process goat cheese and fresh basil with a touch of olive oil, salt, and pepper in a food processor until smooth. Spread on split focaccia and add layers of roasted red bell pepper and arugula. Cut into finger-size sandwiches. We served a similar focaccia sandwich at Johnston Street Café.

Panna Cotta with Balsamic Berries

The Italian translation of "panna cotta" is cooked cream. My friend Bonnie Bailey makes wonderful panna cotta. In fact, I believe this is her recipe.

2 teaspoons unflavored
 gelatin (1 packet)
3 tablespoons cold water
3 cups heavy cream
2 cups plain whole yogurt
2 teaspoons vanilla extract
Seeds from 1 vanilla bean
3/4 cup sugar
8 cups sliced strawberries,
 raspberries and
 blueberries
6 tablespoons balsamic
 vinegar
3 tablespoons sugar
1/2 teaspoon pepper
Freshly grated lemon zest

Soften the gelatin in the cold water in a small bowl. Place the bowl in a larger bowl of hot water. Stir and let stand for 10 minutes or until the gelatin dissolves. Whisk 1 1/2 cups of the cream, the yogurt, vanilla and vanilla bean seeds together in a bowl. Heat the remaining 1 1/2 cups cream and 3/4 cup sugar in a small saucepan. Bring to a simmer over medium heat. Remove from the heat. Stir in the softened gelatin until dissolved. Pour into the yogurt mixture and mix well. Pour into a mold or bowl lined with plastic wrap. Chill, uncovered, until chilled through. Cover with plastic wrap and chill for 8 to 10 hours or until set. Combine the berries, balsamic vinegar, 3 tablespoons sugar and the pepper in a bowl and toss well. Let stand at room temperature for 30 to 60 minutes before serving. To serve, invert the panna cotta onto an elevated cake plate or platter and remove the plastic wrap. Surround with the undrained berries. Dust lightly with the lemon zest and serve.

Yield: 8 to 10 servings

Italian Herb Breadsticks

1/4 cup (1 ounce) grated
 Parmesan cheese
2 1/2 teaspoons Italian
 seasoning
1 teaspoon garlic powder
1 pound frozen bread
 dough, thawed
2 tablespoons butter or
 margarine, melted
1 tablespoon kosher salt

Mix the cheese, Italian seasoning and garlic powder in a bowl. Cut the dough into 24 pieces. Roll each piece into a 12-inch rope. Sprinkle evenly with the cheese mixture. Place the ropes 1 inch apart on lightly greased baking sheets. Let rise, covered with plastic wrap, at room temperature for 20 minutes. Bake at 350 degrees for 15 minutes or until golden brown. Brush the breadsticks with the butter and sprinkle with the salt. Let cool on wire racks for 10 minutes.

Yield: 2 dozen breadsticks

A Supper on the Porch

Menu

Wild Mushroom Pâté

Grilled Flank Steak with Molasses Barbecue Glaze

Spinach Salad with Berries

Caramelized Onion-Stuffed Potatoes

Basil Pesto

Basil Tomato Tart

Parmesan Cheese Muffins

Easy Peach Cobbler

Porch suppers are so much fun—the way most people prefer to entertain and to be entertained these days. Try to prepare as much of the menu as possible the day before. The Wild Mushroom Pâté can be stirred up two or three days before the supper. Spinach (be sure to get tender baby spinach) can be washed and put into sealable plastic bags the day before and stored in the refrigerator. The stuffed potatoes lend themselves nicely to being put together several days in advance and frozen. Remove from the freezer a couple of hours before baking. The Basil Tomato Tart, the muffins, and the Easy Peach Cobbler can be prepared late in the afternoon. Set up your food table along with a casual basket arrangement of zinnias, (or refer to decorating ideas on page 180). Sangria is always a nice addition, or try a nonalcoholic punch, along with a tray of ice water. Guests can be seated at tables or can hold lap trays. Anything goes, but don't forget the candles for later in the evening. I fondly remember going to Sewanee, Tennessee to present a Porch Supper program to the Assembly, and my good friends Carolyn Tweedy and Sally Smart were so supportive.

Wild Mushroom Pâté

1¹/2 pounds mixed wild and
   white domestic
   mushrooms
¹/2 cup (1 stick) unsalted
   butter
16 ounces cream cheese,
   softened
1 teaspoon minced garlic
¹/2 teaspoon thyme
¹/2 teaspoon cayenne pepper
¹/2 teaspoon white pepper
Salt to taste

Sauté the mushrooms in the butter in a skillet until soft. Drain most of the liquid. Process the sautéed mushrooms, cream cheese, garlic, thyme, cayenne pepper, white pepper and salt in a food processor until smooth. Spoon into a serving bowl or crock. Serve with caramelized onions and crostini or pita chips.

Yield: 25 cocktail servings

Grilled Flank Steak with Molasses Barbecue Glaze

*Other inexpensive but delicious cuts of beef include skirt
steak (increasingly popular), brisket, and short ribs. The brisket and short ribs
benefit from long cooking times in a sauce or liquid.*

¹/2 cup molasses
¹/4 cup coarse-grained
   mustard
1 tablespoon olive oil
1 (1¹/2-pound) flank steak

Whisk the molasses, mustard and olive oil together in a bowl. Place the steak in a large sealable plastic bag. Reserve ¹/4 cup of the molasses mixture for basting. Pour the remaining molasses mixture over the steak. Seal tightly and marinate, covered, in the refrigerator for 2 hours, turning occasionally. Drain the steak, discarding the marinade. Place the steak on a grill rack. Grill, covered, over medium-high heat (350 to 400 degrees) for 6 minutes on each side or to the desired degree of doneness, basting frequently with the reserved marinade. Cut the steak diagonally across the grain into very thin strips.

Yield: 6 servings

*Marcona almonds are
Spain's most prized
possession in the form of a
smooth, tan almond. It is
sweet and soft and is
known as the Queen of
Almonds. Warning:
These are addictive. They
go well with almost any
cheese. Great addition
for nibbling with cheese,
olives, and wine. They are
quite the rage and I use
them in salads.*

Spinach Salad with Berries

Berries begin to deteriorate when they are washed.
Wait to wash until just before serving.

10 ounces fresh spinach
 (about 10 cups)
Nonfat Curry Dressing
 (below)
2 cups thickly sliced
 strawberries
1 cup blueberries
1 small red onion,
 thinly sliced
1 cup chopped pecans

Rinse the spinach and pat dry. Tear into bite-size pieces and place in a salad bowl. Add the dressing and toss lightly. Add the berries, onion and pecans and toss lightly.

Yield: 8 to 10 servings

Nonfat Curry Dressing

1/4 cup balsamic vinegar
1/4 cup rice vinegar
3 tablespoons honey
2 teaspoons curry powder
2 teaspoons Dijon mustard
Salt and pepper to taste

Whisk the balsamic vinegar, rice vinegar, honey, curry powder, mustard, salt and pepper together in a bowl.

Yield: about 3/4 cup

Caramelized Onion-Stuffed Potatoes

4 baking potatoes
   (about 3 pounds)
1¹/2 cups (6 ounces)
   shredded Gruyère cheese
5 tablespoons sour cream
1/2 teaspoon salt
1/4 teaspoon freshly ground
   black pepper
5 teaspoons butter
5 cups vertically sliced
   red onion
5 teaspoons sugar
5 tablespoons dry sherry
2 teaspoons Worcestershire
   sauce
1 teaspoon dried thyme
2 garlic cloves, minced

Scrub the potatoes and pierce with a fork.
Place on microwave-safe paper towels in the
microwave. Microwave on High for 10 minutes
or until cooked through, rearranging
the potatoes after 5 minutes. Let stand for
5 minutes. Cut each potato into halves
lengthwise. Scoop out the pulp, leaving a
1/4-inch-thick shell. Combine the potato pulp,
3/4 cup of the cheese, the sour cream, salt
and pepper in a bowl and mix well. Spoon
evenly into the potato shells. Melt the butter
in a medium nonstick skillet over medium-
high heat. Add the onion and sugar. Sauté
for 8 minutes or until brown. Stir in the
sherry, Worcestershire sauce, thyme and garlic.
Cook for 1 minute or until the liquid
evaporates, scraping the skillet to loosen up
the browned bits. Top each potato half with
about 2 tablespoons of the onion mixture and
1¹/2 tablespoons of the remaining cheese.
Arrange the stuffed potato halves in a baking
pan. Bake at 400 degrees until heated through.

Yield: 8 servings

*Easy baked or grilled
whole Vidalia or mild
onions make a great
addition to a menu. Core
the onion and place on a
large piece of foil. Add
1 tablespoon Worcestershire
sauce and 1 tablespoon
butter and fold the foil to
seal. Bake at 350 degrees
for 45 minutes.*

Basil Pesto

3 cups basil leaves
1 cup (4 ounces) shredded
   Parmigiano-Reggiano
   cheese or other
   Parmesan cheese
1/2 cup pine nuts or
   walnuts
3/4 cup (or more) extra-
   virgin olive oil

Process the basil, cheese,
pine nuts and olive oil
in a food processor until
smooth, adding additional
olive oil if needed for the
desired consistency.

Basil Tomato Tart

*If you have extra basil in your garden at the end of the season,
make pesto and freeze in ice cube trays. Then remove and freeze the cubes in a
sealable plastic freezer bag. Pop out anytime you need one to stir
into soup or toss with hot pasta.*

1 baked (9-inch) pie shell
1 1/2 cups (6 ounces)
   shredded mozzarella
   cheese
1/2 cup (2 ounces) grated
   asiago cheese
4 tomatoes
1 cup loosely packed
   fresh basil
4 garlic cloves
1/2 cup mayonnaise
1/4 cup (1 ounce) grated
   Parmesan cheese
1/8 teaspoon white pepper

Sprinkle the warm pie shell with 1/2 cup of the
mozzarella cheese and 1/4 cup of the asiago
cheese. Cut the tomatoes into thin slices and
drain on paper towels. Arrange over the melted
cheese. Process the basil and garlic in a food
processor until finely chopped. Sprinkle over
the tomatoes. Combine the remaining 1 cup
mozzarella cheese, the remaining 1/4 cup asiago
cheese, the mayonnaise, Parmesan cheese and
white pepper in a bowl and mix well. Spread
evenly over the basil and tomatoes. Bake at
350 degrees for 25 minutes or until the top is
golden brown. Serve warm.

Yield: 6 to 8 servings

Parmesan Cheese Muffins

Do not overmix any muffin batter. Use good Parmesan cheese.

2 cups self-rising flour
3/4 cup (3 ounces) shredded
   Parmesan cheese
2 tablespoons sugar
1 cup milk
1/4 cup vegetable oil
2 eggs

Mix the flour, cheese and sugar in a large bowl and make a well in the center. Whisk the milk, oil and eggs together in a bowl until blended. Add to the flour mixture and stir just until moistened. Spoon into lightly greased muffin cups, filling two-thirds full. Bake at 400 degrees for 15 to 18 minutes or until golden brown.

Yield: 1 dozen muffins

Easy Peach Cobbler

This is my special friend Pat Owens' recipe. So great and easy. You can prepare it at the last minute as an emergency dessert.

1/2 cup (1 stick) butter
1 cup all-purpose flour
1 teaspoon baking powder
1 cup sugar
1 cup milk
1 teaspoon vanilla extract
1/4 teaspoon nutmeg
1 teaspoon cinnamon
4 cups undrained freshly
   sliced peaches

Place the butter in a deep 2-quart baking dish. Bake at 325 degrees until the butter melts. Mix the flour, baking powder and sugar in a bowl. Add the milk, vanilla, nutmeg and cinnamon and mix well. Pour into the melted butter. Spoon the peaches over the batter. Do not stir. Bake for 1 hour. Serve with vanilla bean ice cream.

Yield: 8 servings

Cobbler Alternative

Try this cobbler with blackberries or blueberries anytime of the year. You can freeze any kind of berry just off the vine or from the farmers' market. Spread the berries in a single layer on a baking sheet lined with waxed paper. Place in the freezer and freeze until firm. Place the frozen berries in a sealable freezer bag and store in the freezer. Freezing the berries separately will prevent clumping.

A Festive Open House

Menu

Sparkling Pomegranate Cocktail
New Orleans Cocktail Nuts
Mini Flank Steak Rolls
Panko-Crusted Crab Cake Bites
Asparagus Rolls with Three Cheeses
Herbed Crostini
Baked Santa Fe Dip
Cucumber Rounds with Hummus and Sour Cream Topping
White Chocolate and Lime Cheesecake Bars

*I*nvite a crowd for a mouthwatering spread of Southern appetizers. When we visit the Wortheys in Ketchum, Idaho, Jan and I have their friends over for a wide array of cocktail food. This menu could be used anytime of the year. If you've never been to Idaho, especially Ketchum and Sun Valley, you must go sometime. It is a beautiful place among the mountains, and the temperature is usually "just right" in the summer.

This menu starts with a Sparkling Pomegranate Cocktail. The flank steak can be grilled early or mid-afternoon and kept warm. Do not overcook, as the meat will be tough. Medium-rare is good. The Béarnaise Sauce can be made early in the day and kept warm in an insulated bottle. Use cocktail rolls you've purchased. Panko-Crusted Crab Cake Bites are easily made early, covered, and refrigerated until you bake them. Do remove from the refrigerator about an hour before baking. Roasted Pepper Aïoli can be made the day before. Cucumber Rounds are easily assembled, and the White Chocolate and Lime Cheesecake Bars can be prepared two days in advance and refrigerated.

Don't forget a tray for ice water and a wine bar for other drinks. Pass the hors d'oeuvre. Refer to page 180 for decorations. And have fun!

Sparkling Pomegranate Cocktail

Boiled peanuts, easily bought, are considered "Southern edamame,"
a perfect accompaniment to cocktails.

1¹/2 ounces pomegranate
   juice
1 ounce pomegranate syrup
1 ounce pomegranate
   liqueur
4 ounces chilled Champagne
Pomegranate seeds
   for garnish

Combine the pomegranate juice, pomegranate
syrup and pomegranate liqueur in a chilled
Champagne flute. Add the Champagne.
Garnish with pomegranate seeds.

Yield: 1 cocktail

New Orleans Cocktail Nuts

¹/3 cup sugar
¹/4 cup (¹/2 stick)
   unsalted butter
¹/4 cup orange juice
2 teaspoons Cajun seasoning
¹/4 teaspoon cayenne pepper
4 cups pecan halves

Line a rimmed baking sheet with foil and
spray with nonstick cooking spray. Combine
the sugar, butter, orange juice, Cajun seasoning
and cayenne pepper in a heavy skillet and
mix well. Cook until the sugar dissolves,
stirring constantly. Stir in the pecans to coat.
Spread on the prepared baking sheet. Bake
at 250 degrees for 1 hour, stirring every 15 to
20 minutes. Let cool on the baking sheet.
Break into chunks and store in an airtight
container at room temperature.

Yield: 4 cups

Mini Flank Steak Rolls

We are using less expensive beef now, but it's just as tasty.

1/4 cup sliced fresh ginger
5 garlic cloves
1 (12-ounce) can cola
1 cup (packed) brown sugar
1/2 cup torn fresh cilantro
1/4 cup soy sauce
1 tablespoon pepper
1 1/2 pounds flank steak
3 1/2 cups shredded lettuce
Béarnaise Sauce (below)
24 cocktail rolls, split

Crush the ginger and garlic in a large sealable plastic bag. Add the cola, brown sugar, cilantro, soy sauce, pepper and steak. Seal tightly and marinate for 30 minutes. Drain the steak, discarding the marinade. Place the steak on a grill rack. Grill over high heat for 5 minutes on each side for medium-rare. Remove from the grill and let stand for 5 minutes. Slice the steak thinly across the grain. Layer the lettuce, steak and Béarnaise Sauce on the bottom half of each roll. Top with the top half.

Yield: 24 rolls

Béarnaise Sauce

1 tablespoon chopped
    shallots or scallions
1 small sprig of tarragon, or
    1 teaspoon dried tarragon
Pinch of salt
1/4 cup white wine
1/4 cup tarragon vinegar
1 cup (2 sticks) butter
6 egg yolks
3/4 teaspoon salt
Pinch of cayenne pepper
Juice of 1 1/2 lemons

Mix the shallots, tarragon, pinch of salt, the wine and vinegar in a skillet. Simmer until all of the liquid has evaporated and set aside. Place the butter in a microwave-safe dish. Microwave on High for 2 minutes. Microwave until the butter is melted and bubbly. Process the egg yolks, 3/4 teaspoon salt, the cayenne pepper and lemon juice in a food processor or blender until smooth. Add the hot butter and process until thickened. Add the tarragon mixture and mix well. Pour into an insulated bottle to keep warm.

Yield: about 1 1/2 cups

Panko-Crusted Crab Cake Bites

These are always popular. Be sure to make plenty of extras.

1/4 cup finely chopped celery
1 tablespoon minced
  fresh chives
1/4 cup mayonnaise
1 egg
1 teaspoon Dijon mustard
1/4 teaspoon hot pepper sauce
12 ounces shelled cooked
  crab meat, flaked
1 1/4 cups panko or fine dried
  bread crumbs
Roasted Pepper-Chive Aïoli
  (below)
Fresh chives, cut into 1-inch
  lengths for garnish

Combine the celery, minced chives, mayonnaise, egg, Dijon mustard and hot sauce in a bowl and mix well with a fork. Add the crab meat and 1/4 cup of the panko and stir gently. Place the remaining 1 cup panko in a shallow bowl. Shape the crab mixture into twenty-four cakes about 2 inches wide and 1/2 inch thick. Dredge each cake in the panko, turning to coat all sides and pressing gently to adhere. Place the cakes slightly apart in an oiled 12×17-inch baking pan. Bake at 475 degrees for 15 to 18 minutes or until golden brown. Remove the cakes to a platter with a spatula. Spoon a dollop of Roasted Pepper-Chive Aïoli onto each cake. Garnish with fresh chives. Serve hot.

Yield: 24 crab cake bites

Roasted Pepper-Chive Aïoli

1/4 cup drained canned
  roasted red peppers
1/3 cup mayonnaise
1 tablespoon minced
  fresh chives
2 teaspoons lemon juice
1 teaspoon minced garlic

Chop the red peppers. Process with the mayonnaise, chives, lemon juice and garlic in a food processor until smooth.

Yield: about 1/2 cup

Asparagus Rolls with Three Cheeses

How tasty with three cheeses!

10 fresh asparagus spears
4 ounces blue cheese
2 ounces cream cheese, softened
1/4 cup (1/2 stick) unsalted butter, softened
1 teaspoon grated onion
10 slices thin white bread, crusts trimmed
1/4 cup (1/2 stick) unsalted butter, melted
1/2 cup (2 ounces) grated Parmigiano-Reggiano cheese

Blanch the asparagus in boiling water in a saucepan for 3 to 5 minutes. Plunge into ice water to stop the cooking process. Drain and pat dry. Process the blue cheese, cream cheese, softened butter and onion in a food processor until smooth. Roll each slice of bread 1/8 inch thick. Spread each with the cheese mixture. Place an asparagus spear in the center of each and roll up. Trim any asparagus that extends beyond the end of the bread. Brush the roll-ups with the melted butter and coat with the Parmesan-Reggiano cheese. Place on a baking sheet. Bake at 350 degrees for 15 to 20 minutes or until golden brown. Cut into thirds to serve.

Yield: 30 rolls

Herbed Crostini

1/2 cup (1 stick) unsalted butter, melted
1/2 cup olive oil
1/2 teaspoon minced garlic
1 tablespoon chopped fresh dill weed, chives, thyme and rosemary
1 package unsliced hoagie buns, sliced 1/4 inch thick

Combine the butter, olive oil, garlic and herbs in a bowl and mix well. Brush each side of the baguette slices with the herb mixture. Arrange on a baking sheet lined with foil or baking parchment. Bake at 250 degrees for 45 minutes or until crispy. Let cool on a wire rack. Store in sealable plastic freezer bags in the freezer.

Yield: 4 dozen

For a fun, tongue-in-cheek Southern appetizer to serve with drinks, serve pork rinds in silver bowls.

Baked Santa Fe Dip

2 cups (8 ounces) shredded
   Cheddar cheese
1 cup (4 ounces) shredded
   Monterey Jack cheese or
   mozzarella cheese
1/2 cup light mayonnaise
1 (8-ounce) can whole kernel
   corn, drained (3/4 cup)
1 (4-ounce) can chopped
   green chiles, drained
2 teaspoons finely chopped
   canned chipotle chiles in
   adobo sauce
1/2 teaspoon garlic powder
1 tomato, seeded and
   chopped (3/4 cup)
1/4 cup sliced green onions
2 tablespoons chopped
   fresh cilantro

Combine the Cheddar cheese, Monterey Jack cheese, mayonnaise, corn, green chiles, chipotle chiles and garlic powder in a large bowl and mix well. Spread in a 9-inch baking dish or shallow 1-quart baking dish. Chill, covered, for up to 24 hours. Place the tomato, green onions and cilantro in a bowl and mix well. Chill, covered, until serving time. To serve, bake the cheese mixture at 350 degrees for 25 minutes or until heated through. Spoon the tomato mixture in the center. Serve with vegetables and tortilla chips. You may substitute 2 teaspoons minced jalapeño chiles for the chipotle chiles.

Yield: 28 servings

Cucumber Rounds with Hummus and Sour Cream Topping

So healthy.

1 (15-ounce) can chick-peas, drained and rinsed
1 large garlic clove, coarsely chopped
3 tablespoons fresh lemon juice
3 tablespoons tahini (mixed well before measuring)
2 tablespoons extra-virgin olive oil
1 teaspoon ground cumin
1/4 teaspoon kosher salt or sea salt
2 tablespoons water
1 large seedless cucumber
Kosher salt or sea salt and pepper to taste
1/4 cup sour cream
2 tablespoons sesame seeds, toasted

Process the chick-peas, garlic, lemon juice, tahini, olive oil, cumin, 1/4 teaspoon salt and the water in a food processor for 2 minutes or until smooth. Peel the cucumber lengthwise at 1/4-inch intervals to create a striped pattern using a vegetable peeler. Cut the cucumber crosswise into 1/4-inch rounds and place on a platter. Add salt and pepper to the sour cream and mix well. Top each round with a generous teaspoon of the hummus and a dollop of the sour cream. Sprinkle with the sesame seeds.

Yield: about 40 rounds

White Chocolate and Lime Cheesecake Bars

These are so refreshing and yummy.

7 ounces good-quality white chocolate (such as Lindt), chopped

27 chocolate sandwich cookies (about 11 ounces)

1/2 cup heavy whipping cream, chilled

8 ounces cream cheese, softened

3 tablespoons sugar

3 tablespoons fresh lime juice

1 tablespoon finely grated lime zest

White chocolate curls for garnish

Lime slices or lime twists for garnish

Line an 8×8-inch baking pan with foil, extending the foil over each side. Place the white chocolate in a small metal bowl. Heat over barely simmering water in a saucepan until melted and smooth, stirring constantly. Remove the bowl from over the hot water. Process the cookies in a food processor until finely ground. Add 2 tablespoons of the melted white chocolate and mix until the mixture clumps together. Press firmly in the prepared pan. Chill in the refrigerator. Beat the whipping cream in a medium bowl until firm peaks form. Beat the cream cheese, sugar, lime juice and lime zest in a large mixing bowl until smooth. Beat in the remaining melted white chocolate. Fold in the whipped cream one-half at a time. Spread over the prepared crust. Chill for at least 2 hours or until slightly firm. Lift out of the pan using the foil extensions as an aid. Cut into bars. Garnish with white chocolate curls and lime slices.

Yield: 9 bars

Buy chocolate cordial cups and fill with Lemon Curd (page 167).

A Celebration Feast

Menu

Champagne Punch

Mini Shrimp Puffs

Pear and Mesclun Salad with Candied Walnuts

Beef Tenderloin with Cognac Sauce

Three-Cheese Potato Gratin

Green Beans with Orange Essence and Toasted Maple Pecans

Yeast Rolls

Cherries Jubilee

At the Sims home, this Celebration Feast is always on Christmas evening. I love having the entire family for this special day. We open gifts late in the day, always anticipated by all of the grandchildren, followed by dinner. As for nibblers, I keep them light—perhaps marcona almonds and the Shrimp Puffs or a simple dip with scoops. I do pull out all of the china, crystal, and silver to make this a true celebration.

One of my favorite salads is the Pear and Mesclun Salad; the walnuts can be prepared in advance. The meat is seared to perfection by Dr. Bill. He uses a simple marinade. The meat will hold for an hour or so after grilling, before serving, covered by foil. This Cognac Sauce may be made ahead and reheated. I prepare the Potato Gratin and refrigerate the day before. The Green Beans may be put together an hour or so before dinner. Leave off the Maple Pecans if you are pushed for time. Use Sister Schubert Rolls or Jo Hosey's rolls if you have no time to make your own. Of course, yours can be precooked and frozen.

The crowning glory of this meal is the flaming Cherries Jubilee, served over vanilla bean ice cream. I also have a variety of other desserts for the children. This meal could be served to celebrate any great occasion. The Christmas Feast offered in my classes is always filled immediately. Greg Clemons does the stripping and roasting of the meat.

Champagne Punch

2 cups cranberry juice
  cocktail
1 (12-ounce) can frozen
  orange juice concentrate,
  thawed
1 cup lemon juice
1 cup sugar
1 (375-milliliter) bottle
  sauterne or dessert wine
2 (750-milliliter) bottles
  Champagne, chilled
Ice Ring (below)

Combine the cranberry juice cocktail, orange juice concentrate, lemon juice and sugar in a pitcher and mix well. Chill for 8 hours or longer. Pour into a chilled punch bowl. Stir in the sauterne and Champagne gently just before serving. Float the Ice Ring fruit side up in the punch.

Yield: 20 servings

Ice Ring

1 1/2 to 2 cups orange juice
1/2 cup cranberry juice
6 to 8 seedless red
  grape clusters
10 to 12 orange slices, seeded
8 to 10 whole strawberries
Sprigs of fresh mint

Combine the orange juice and cranberry juice in a pitcher. Line the bottom of a 6-cup ring mold with the grape clusters and one-half of the orange slices, using the grapes to stand the orange slices vertically. Pour a thin layer of the juice mixture into the mold. Freeze for 2 hours or until firm. Arrange the remaining orange slices, the strawberries and mint around the grapes. Pour the remaining juice mixture around the fruit filling almost to the top of the mold. Freeze for 8 hours. Unmold by dipping the bottom half of the mold into several inches of warm water for 5 to 10 seconds to loosen, repeating as necessary to release the ring. Do not immerse the entire mold in water. Invert the ring onto a plate.

Yield: 1 ice ring

Mini Shrimp Puffs

1/4 cup cornstarch
1 1/4 cups milk
2 eggs
2 egg yolks
1 cup heavy cream
1/2 teaspoon kosher salt
Pinch of cayenne pepper
1/2 cup (2 ounces) grated
    Parmigiano-Reggiano
    cheese
Canned or frozen tiny
    cooked cocktail shrimp
1 to 2 tablespoons finely
    chopped fresh herbs, such
    as basil, chives, dill weed,
    or flat-leaf parsley

Place the cornstarch in a medium bowl. Whisk in 1/2 cup of the milk gradually until smooth. Whisk in the eggs and egg yolks until smooth. Whisk in the remaining milk, cream, salt and cayenne pepper. Place 1/2 teaspoon of the cheese, 3 tiny shrimp and a pinch of fresh herbs in each of forty-eight buttered or oiled miniature muffin cups. Add 2 tablespoons of the batter to each. Bake at 400 degrees on a rack in the upper third of the oven for 15 to 18 minutes or until the clafoutis puff and begin to turn golden brown. Let cool in the pan on a wire rack for 20 minutes. Run a paring knife carefully around the rim of each muffin cup to loosen. Lift carefully out of each cup and serve.

Yield: 48 hors d'oeuvres

Pear and Mesclun Salad with Candied Walnuts

The driest salad greens produce the best salad because the dressing sticks to the greens. Dry your greens in a salad spinner or place in a clean cotton pillowcase with paper towels layered inside. Store in the refrigerator in the pillowcase until needed.

1 pound mesclun or mixed
   salad greens
Balsamic vinaigrette
2 firm ripe pears, cut into
   halves and thinly sliced
   lengthwise
Candied Walnuts (below)

Place the mesclun on a serving platter. Drizzle with vinaigrette. Arrange the pear slices over the top and sprinkle with Candied Walnuts.

Yield: 8 servings

Candied Walnuts

1 cup walnut pieces
   (3 to 4 ounces)
2 tablespoons light
   corn syrup
1 tablespoon sugar
1/2 teaspoon salt
1/4 teaspoon ground
   black pepper
Generous pinch of
   cayenne pepper

Combine the walnuts, corn syrup, sugar, salt, black pepper and cayenne pepper in a bowl and mix well. Spread on a baking sheet sprayed with nonstick cooking spray. Bake at 325 degrees for 15 minutes or until the walnuts are golden brown and the sugar mixture is bubbly, stirring occasionally to break up any clumps. Let cool completely on the baking sheet. May be prepared three days ahead. Store in an airtight container.

Yield: 1 cup

Beef Tenderloin with Cognac Sauce

Doc has become proficient with this grilling.

1 (6- to 7-pound) fillet
  of beef
1 cup olive oil
1/2 cup red wine
Cracked pepper to taste
2 garlic cloves, minced
Cognac Sauce (below)

Place the beef in a shallow dish. Pour a mixture of the olive oil, wine, pepper and garlic over the beef, turning to coat. Marinate, covered, in the refrigerator for 1 hour, turning occasionally. Rub with additional pepper. Drain the beef, discarding the marinade. Place the beef on a grill rack. Grill over high heat for 5 minutes. Turn and grill for 5 minutes longer. Reduce the grill temperature to medium. Grill for 20 minutes longer or to 140 degrees on a meat thermometer for rare or to 160 degrees for medium. Let stand for 10 minutes before slicing. Serve with Cognac Sauce.

Yield: 10 to 12 servings

Pay the butcher to trim your tenderloin. Ask him to fold and tie the tail for even roasting.

Cognac Sauce

2 tablespoons butter
2 tablespoons minced shallot
2 tablespoons minced garlic
1/4 teaspoon salt
1/4 teaspoon pepper
1 tablespoon all-purpose
  flour
2 cups beef broth
1/4 cup Cognac
1/4 cup heavy whipping
  cream

Melt the butter in a medium saucepan over medium heat. Add the shallot, garlic, salt and pepper. Cook for 5 to 6 minutes, stirring frequently. Stir in the flour. Cook for 1 minute, stirring constantly. Whisk in the broth and Cognac gradually until smooth. Bring to a simmer. Reduce the heat to low. Cook for 10 minutes, stirring occasionally. Add the cream. Simmer for 10 minutes or until slightly thickened, stirring occasionally.

Yield: about 3 cups

Three-Cheese Potato Gratin

2 pounds Yukon Gold
   potatoes or russet
   potatoes, peeled and
   cut into 1/8-inch slices
1 1/2 cups heavy cream
1 1/2 cups milk
1 teaspoon coarse salt
1/8 teaspoon freshly
   ground pepper
Generous pinch of freshly
   grated nutmeg
2 garlic cloves, crushed
1/2 cup (2 ounces) freshly
   grated Parmigiano-
   Reggiano cheese
1 cup (4 ounces) shredded
   Gruyère cheese or
   Swiss cheese
2 ounces fresh goat cheese,
   crumbled

Combine the potatoes, cream, milk, salt,
pepper, nutmeg and garlic in a large heavy
saucepan and mix well. Bring to a boil over
medium-high heat, stirring occasionally.
Remove the garlic cloves. Pour the potato
mixture into a 2 1/2- or 3-quart baking dish.
Top with the Parmigiano-Reggiano cheese,
Gruyère cheese and goat cheese. Bake at
400 degrees for 40 minutes or until the top
is a deep golden brown and the potatoes
are very tender when pierced with a knife.
Remove from the oven and let cool for
15 minutes or until warm or serve at room
temperature. Use part beef broth for the
heavy cream to reduce calories. Buy whole
nutmeg and grate as needed with a microplane.

Yield: 6 to 8 servings

Green Beans with Orange Essence and Toasted Maple Pecans

Use small green beans (haricots verts) for an elegant dish.

3/4 cup pecans, chopped
  (about 1 3/4 ounces)
3 tablespoons unsalted butter
2 tablespoons maple syrup
1/8 teaspoon salt
2 shallots, minced
  (about 1/2 cup)
1/2 teaspoon grated
  orange zest
Pinch of cayenne pepper
1 teaspoon all-purpose flour
2/3 cup low-sodium chicken
  broth
1/3 cup orange juice
1 1/2 pounds small green
  beans, trimmed
1 teaspoon minced fresh
  sage leaves
Salt and black pepper
  to taste

Heat the pecans in a 12-inch nonstick skillet over medium-high heat for 3 minutes or until fragrant, stirring occasionally. Turn off the heat. Stir in 1 tablespoon of the butter, the maple syrup and 1/8 teaspoon salt. Cook over medium heat for 45 seconds or until the pecans are dry and glossy, stirring constantly. Remove to a plate and set aside. Wipe out the skillet and add the remaining 2 tablespoons butter. Heat over medium heat until the foaming subsides. Add the shallots, orange zest and cayenne pepper. Cook for 2 minutes or until the shallots are softened, stirring occasionally. Stir in the flour. Add the broth and orange juice. Add the green beans and toss to coat. Increase the heat to medium-high. Cook, covered, for 4 minutes or until the green beans are partly tender but still crisp at the center. Cook, uncovered, for 4 minutes longer or until the green beans are tender and the sauce is slightly thickened. Remove from the heat. Add the sage, salt and black pepper to taste. Spoon into a serving dish. Sprinkle evenly with the pecans.

Yield: 8 servings

Yeast Rolls

1 cup water
1/2 cup (1 stick) butter or
  margarine
1/2 cup shortening
3/4 cup sugar
1 1/2 teaspoons salt
2 envelopes dry yeast
1 cup lukewarm water
2 eggs, lightly beaten
6 cups (about) all-purpose
  flour
Melted butter

Bring 1 cup water to a boil in a saucepan.
Remove from the heat. Add 1/2 cup butter and
the shortening and stir until melted. Stir in
the sugar and salt. Let stand until lukewarm.
Dissolve the yeast in 1 cup lukewarm water in
a large bowl. Add the butter mixture and eggs
and mix well. Stir in just enough flour to make
a stiff dough. Chill, covered, for 8 to 10 hours.
Roll the dough on a lightly floured surface
1/4 to 1/3 inch thick. Cut with a biscuit cutter
and fold in half. Place in a greased baking pan.
Brush with melted butter. Let rise in a warm
place for 1 1/2 to 2 hours or until doubled in
bulk. Bake at 400 degrees for 12 to 15 minutes
or until brown.

Yield: 8 dozen rolls

Cherries Jubilee

Be sure to use brandy or kirsch with a high enough alcohol content to flame.

1 (15-ounce) can pitted
  black sweet cherries
1 tablespoon sugar
1 tablespoon cornstarch
1 teaspoon cinnamon
1/4 cup warmed kirsch
  or brandy
Vanilla bean ice cream

Drain the cherries, reserving 1 cup of the juice.
Mix the sugar, cornstarch and cinnamon in
a saucepan. Stir in the reserved juice a small
amount at a time. Cook for 3 minutes, stirring
constantly. Stir in the cherries. Pour the warm
kirsch over the top. Ignite and let the flames
subside. Serve immediately over vanilla bean
ice cream. This recipe may be doubled.

Yield: 6 servings

Southern Scrumptious Favorites

Contents

I hope you enjoy the medley of recipes contained in this section. If you want to substitute some of these recipes for some found in the menu section, please do so. For instance, if you do not love brussels sprouts, substitute beans or asparagus.

Many friends and family have shared recipes with me, and they are featured in this section, along with some of my own favorites. We have traveled extensively through the years, and I have gleaned recipes from other U.S. cities and abroad. France and Italy are special favorites.

In the back of the book are helpful guides for organizing for entertaining, planning an appetizer buffet, how to set up a bar, and food quantities for serving twenty-five, fifty, and one hundred people.

My favorite thing is cooking for family and friends. I hope this book will give you confidence to make my favorite thing yours too!

Smoked Salmon and Fingerling Potatoes

These fingerling potatoes provide various shapes and are tasty with the smoked salmon. Add a little black caviar on top of the crème fraîche to add an elegant touch.

12 fingerling potatoes, cut into halves lengthwise (about 1 pound)
1¹/2 tablespoons extra-virgin olive oil
¹/2 cup crème fraîche or sour cream
Salt and cracked pepper to taste
4 ounces thinly sliced smoked salmon
1 tablespoon caviar or capers

Toss the potatoes with the olive oil on a rimmed baking sheet and spread in a single layer. Bake at 425 degrees for 20 minutes or until tender and golden brown. Remove from the oven to cool. Mix the crème fraîche with salt and pepper in a bowl. Arrange pieces of smoked salmon on each potato and add a dollop of the crème fraîche. Top with the caviar.

Yield: 2 dozen

Smoked Conecuh Sausage in Puff Pastry

6 Conecuh sausages
1 sheet puff pastry
1 egg
2 tablespoons water
Dip for Smoked Conecuh Sausage in Puff Pastry (at right)

Sauté the sausages in a skillet for 10 minutes or until cooked through. Remove from the heat to cool. Roll the puff pastry into a rectangle. Cut into six pieces. Wrap the pastry around each sausage. Brush with a mixture of the egg and water. Place on a lined baking sheet. Bake at 400 degrees for 15 minutes or until brown. Cut into slices and serve with the dip.

Yield: 18 pieces

Dip for Smoked Conecuh Sausage in Puff Pastry

2 cups seedless plum or raspberry marmalade
1 tablespoon prepared horseradish
1 tablespoon Worcestershire sauce
1/4 cup cider vinegar
1 teaspoon ground cinnamon
1 teaspoon vanilla extract

Combine the marmalade, horseradish, Worcestershire sauce, vinegar, cinnamon and vanilla in a bowl and mix well. Spoon into a small bowl for dipping.

Yield: about 2¹/2 cups

Praline Bacon

1 pound bacon
3 tablespoons sugar
1 1/2 teaspoons
   chili powder
1/4 cup finely
   chopped pecans

Arrange the bacon in a
single layer on a rack in
a broiler pan. Bake at
425 degrees on the middle
oven rack for 10 minutes.
Sprinkle with a mixture of
the sugar and chili powder.
Top with the pecans. Bake
for 5 minutes or until
crisp. Use as a topping for
polenta or use just as an
appetizer stacked like
"Lincoln Logs."

Yield: 8 servings

Maple-Glazed Bacon on Gorgonzola Polenta Squares

*This sounds like trouble, but if you make the polenta the day
before and chill, it is a breeze to make.*

1 1/2 cups milk
1 1/2 cups low-sodium
   chicken broth
1/2 teaspoon salt
1 cup polenta
3/4 cup coarsely crumbled
   Gorgonzola cheese or
   other blue cheese
1 pound thick-cut
   applewood-smoked bacon
1 cup packed light
   brown sugar
1/2 cup walnuts
1/4 cup pure maple syrup

Bring the milk, broth and salt to a boil in a
heavy medium saucepan over medium-high
heat. Whisk in the polenta gradually. Reduce
the heat to medium-low. Cook for 15 minutes
or until the polenta is thick enough to come
away from the side of the pan, stirring
constantly. Stir in the cheese. Spread evenly
in a 9×9-inch dish. Chill for 2 to 24 hours
or until cold and firm. Arrange the bacon in
a single layer on a lined rimmed baking sheet.
Pulse the brown sugar, walnuts and maple
syrup in a food processor until the walnuts are
chopped and crumbly in texture. Sprinkle over
the bacon. Bake at 250 degrees for 1 hour or
until the topping is caramelized and the bacon
is cooked through but still flexible. Let cool for
10 minutes. Cut the bacon crosswise into
1-inch pieces. Increase the oven temperature
to 350 degrees. Cut the polenta into 1-inch
squares. Place on a lined rimmed baking sheet.
Top each square with a bacon piece. Bake for
10 minutes or until heated through. Place on
a platter and serve hot.

Yield: 8 servings

Crostini with Roasted Garlic, Goat Cheese and Apple Chutney

Make the apple chutney several days ahead and this recipe is a snap.

1 cup packed light
   brown sugar
3/4 cup rice vinegar
2 garlic cloves, minced
1 1/2 teaspoons minced
   peeled fresh ginger
1/8 teaspoon cayenne pepper
1 cinnamon stick
1 1/2 pounds Granny Smith
   apples, peeled and cut
   into 1/4-inch pieces
1 cup golden raisins
1 cup chopped seeded
   plum tomatoes
1 tablespoon chopped
   fresh mint
Herbed Crostini (page 76)
Roasted garlic
12 ounces soft fresh goat
   cheese, at room
   temperature

Cook the brown sugar and vinegar in a large heavy saucepan over medium heat until the brown sugar dissolves, stirring constantly. Add the garlic, ginger, cayenne pepper and cinnamon stick. Simmer for 8 minutes or until the mixture is syrupy and reduced to 1/2 cup. Stir in the apples and raisins. Increase the heat to high. Boil for 10 minutes or until the apples are tender, stirring frequently. Let cool to room temperature. Discard the cinnamon stick. Stir in the tomatoes and mint. Spread each crostini with roasted garlic. Top with the goat cheese and chutney.

Yield: 20 crostini

Meatballs in Peanut Curry Sauce

Meatballs are coming back. This is a particularly tasty recipe.
To save time, you can buy meatballs already prepared in the frozen food
section of the grocery store and make the sauce.

1/2 cup all-purpose flour
1 pound medium-lean
    ground beef
1 1/2 teaspoons salt
1/4 teaspoon freshly
    ground pepper
2 tablespoons canola oil
4 garlic cloves,
    coarsely chopped
1 tablespoon red curry paste
1 cup canned coconut milk
    (use thicker part)
2 tablespoons chunky
    peanut butter
2 teaspoons fish sauce
1 1/2 tablespoons sugar

Place the flour in a sealable plastic bag. Mix the ground beef, salt and pepper in a bowl. Shape into 1-inch balls. Add to the flour and shake to coat. Dust off the excess flour from the meatballs and set aside. Heat the canola oil in a skillet over medium heat. Add the garlic. Sauté for 2 minutes. Remove the garlic from the canola oil and set aside. Increase the heat to high. Add the meatballs to the canola oil in the skillet. Cook for 4 minutes or until evenly brown and cooked through. Remove with a slotted spoon to a paper towel-lined plate. Place the red curry paste in a saucepan over medium-high heat. Add the reserved garlic. Stir in the coconut milk and peanut butter. Cook until smooth, stirring constantly with a wooden spoon. Add the fish sauce and sugar and mix well. Stir in the meatballs.

Yield: 25 meatballs

Burgundy Mushrooms

These are always a great addition to any party. They may be stored in the refrigerator for three weeks.

4 pounds fresh button
   mushrooms
2 cups (4 sticks)
   unsalted butter
1 quart burgundy
1 1/2 tablespoons
   Worcestershire sauce
1 teaspoon dill seed
1 teaspoon pepper
1 teaspoon garlic powder
2 cups boiling water
4 beef bouillon cubes
4 chicken bouillon cubes
2 teaspoons salt, or to taste

Combine the mushrooms, butter, burgundy, Worcestershire sauce, dill seed, pepper, garlic powder, water and bouillon cubes in a large heavy saucepan and mix well. Bring to a slow boil over medium heat. Reduce the heat and simmer, covered, for 5 to 6 hours. Cook, uncovered, until the liquid barely covers the mushrooms. Sprinkle with the salt. Remove from the heat to cool. Chill if not serving immediately. Serve in a chafing dish with picks.

Yield: 12 to 16 servings

Macadamia-Stuffed Mushrooms

*Who does not like crunchy, delicious macadamia nuts?
These mushrooms are outstanding and also can be used as a side dish.*

1 pound white mushrooms
   or baby bella mushrooms
1/2 cup chopped onion
2 tablespoons butter
1/2 cup chopped
   macadamia nuts
1 tablespoon dry white wine
1 teaspoon salt
1/2 teaspoon pepper
1/2 cup bread crumbs

Remove the stems from the mushrooms, reserving the caps. Chop the stems coarsely. Sauté the stems with the onion in the butter in a skillet. Add the macadamia nuts, wine, salt and pepper. Stir in enough of the bread crumbs to bind. Stuff into the reserved mushroom caps. Arrange on a lined baking sheet. Bake at 425 degrees for 10 minutes.

Yield: 12 servings

Parmesan Puffs

This appetizer is very simple and actually adds an elegant touch served as they are popped out of the oven. When we were in medical school eons ago, I served these often because I generally had all ingredients on hand and they were economical to make.

1 onion
1 cup mayonnaise
1 cup (4 ounces) grated
  Parmesan cheese
1 loaf thinly sliced white
  bread (about 30 slices)

Slice the onion into small pieces. Soak the onion in water to cover in a bowl and drain. Mix the mayonnaise and cheese in a bowl. Cut the bread into rounds with a biscuit cutter. Spread each round with the mayonnaise mixture and top with a small piece of onion. Bake at 400 degrees for 10 minutes or just until beginning to brown. Serve hot.

Yield: 30 appetizers

Use Parmigiano-Reggiano cheese, the king of the Parmesan cheeses, if possible. It is made from skimmed cow's milk. It has a hard, pale golden rind, straw-colored interior, and a rich, sharp flavor. It is most often aged for two years. It comes, of course, from Parma, Italy, and surrounding areas.

Blue Cheese Crisps

A nice change from cheese straws or regular cheese biscuits.

8 ounces crumbled
  blue cheese
1/2 cup (1 stick) butter or
  margarine, softened
1 1/3 cups all-purpose flour
1/3 cup poppy seeds
1/4 teaspoon ground
  red pepper

Beat the cheese and butter at medium speed in a mixing bowl until creamy. Add the flour, poppy seeds and red pepper and beat until smooth. Divide the dough into two equal portions. Shape each portion into a 9-inch log. Wrap each log in waxed paper or plastic wrap. Chill, covered, for 2 hours. Cut each log into slices 1/4 inch thick. Place on ungreased baking sheets. Bake at 350 degrees for 13 to 15 minutes or until golden brown. Remove to wire racks to cool completely.

Yield: 6 dozen

Brandied-Raisin Brie

Brie also may be served with either apricot or orange marmalade.
Sprinkle toasted almonds on top.

1/4 cup chopped walnuts
3 tablespoons brandy
1/4 cup golden raisins
1 (8-ounce) wheel or
   wedge Brie cheese

Spread the walnuts in a single layer on an ungreased baking sheet. Bake at 350 degrees for 3 minutes, stirring after 1 1/2 minutes. Watch carefully to prevent overbrowning. Let cool on a paper towel. Place the brandy and raisins in a microwave-safe cup. Microwave, covered loosely with a microwave-safe paper towel, on High for 40 seconds. Place the cheese on a microwave-safe plate. Microwave on High for 40 seconds to soften. Spread the raisin mixture over the top. Sprinkle with the toasted walnuts. Serve warm with an assortment of crackers or bread rounds.

Yield: 8 servings

Beer Cheese Spread

Peggy Burkhart, a longtime friend from Kentucky, sent me
this recipe. Peg and Bill along with Florence and Jere Hornsby,
are friends from medical school.

32 ounces sharp Cheddar
   cheese, shredded
1 small onion, minced
2 garlic cloves, minced
1 teaspoon hot pepper sauce
1/4 teaspoon ground
   red pepper
1 (12-ounce) bottle amber
   beer, at room temperature
Salt and black pepper
   to taste
Sprig of fresh thyme
   for garnish

Beat the cheese, onion, garlic, hot sauce and red pepper at low speed in the bowl of a heavy-duty electric stand mixer until blended. Add the beer gradually, beating well after each addition. Beat at medium speed for 1 minute or until creamy. Add salt and black pepper. Chill, covered, for 2 hours. Garnish with thyme. Store in an airtight container in the refrigerator for up to two weeks.

Yield: 5 cups

Crab and Shrimp Mousse

A popular item at any get-together.

8 ounces cream cheese,
    softened
1 cup mayonnaise
1¹/2 cups salsa
1 envelope unflavored gelatin
¹/4 cup cold water
2 (4-ounce) cans baby shrimp
1 (4-ounce) can lump
    crab meat
Fresh sage or parsley
    for garnish

Process the cream cheese, mayonnaise and salsa in a food processor until smooth. Soften the gelatin in the cold water in a glass measure. Place the glass measure in simmering water in a saucepan. Heat until the gelatin dissolves. Add the gelatin mixture to the cream cheese mixture and mix well. Fold in the shrimp and crab meat. Spoon into a mold or bowl lined with plastic wrap. Chill, covered with plastic wrap, for several hours. Uncover and invert onto a serving plate. Remove the plastic wrap. Garnish with fresh sage or parsley. Serve with crostini or wheat crackers. Pasteurized lump crab meat, located in the refrigerator section of your favorite grocery, may be used.

Yield: 20 cocktail servings

Olive Spread

1 cup pitted green olives,
　 drained and sliced
1 cup pitted black olives,
　 drained and sliced
1 bunch green onions,
　 chopped
1 cup mayonnaise
1 cup (4 ounces) shredded
　 sharp Cheddar cheese
1 cup (4 ounces) shredded
　 Monterey Jack cheese
Dash of Tabasco sauce

Combine the green olives, black olives, green onions, mayonnaise, Cheddar cheese, Monterey Jack cheese and Tabasco sauce in a bowl and mix well. Place in a serving bowl. Chill until serving time. Serve with corn scoops.

Yield: about 4 1/2 cups

Molded Vegetable Spread

This is our family's most favorite appetizer. Each Memorial Day our entire family is in Destin, Florida, and Seaside. It is a tradition to have this recipe. It is gobbled up in no time on tiny wheat crackers as we all "camp" around the hors d'oeuvre table. My sister, Catherine, makes the best. It also can be used as a sandwich spread.

2 tomatoes, finely chopped
1 cup finely chopped celery
1 small onion, finely chopped
1 bell pepper, finely chopped
1 cucumber, finely chopped
1 envelope unflavored gelatin
1/4 cup cold water
1/4 cup boiling water
1 pint mayonnaise
1 teaspoon salt

Drain the tomatoes, celery, onion, bell pepper and cucumber on paper towels. Soften the gelatin in cold water in a large bowl. Add the boiling water and stir until dissolved. Let stand until cool. Fold in the mayonnaise and salt. Add the vegetables and mix well. Place in a 1-quart bowl or mold lined with plastic wrap. Chill until set. Unmold onto a serving platter and remove the plastic wrap. Serve with crackers, crostini or bread.

Yield: 12 to 15 servings

Creamy Collard Dip

Very similar to a spinach dip, but my goodness, who would have ever thought we'd see collards at a cocktail party? Collards are available in most markets year round. They are an excellent source of vitamins A and C, calcium, and iron.

6 slices bacon
1 small sweet onion,
　chopped (about 1 cup)
1 red bell pepper, chopped
　(3/4 cup)
8 ounces fresh collard
　greens, trimmed and
　coarsely chopped (6 cups)
3 garlic cloves, minced
8 ounces cream cheese, cut
　into cubes and softened
2 cups (8 ounces) shredded
　Monterey Jack cheese
1/2 cup light cream
1/2 teaspoon Cajun
　seasoning (optional)
Thin breadsticks or vegetable
　dippers, such as red
　bell pepper strips

Cook the bacon in a 12-inch skillet until crisp. Remove the bacon to paper towels to drain. Drain the skillet, reserving 2 teaspoons of the bacon drippings. Add the onion and bell pepper to the reserved drippings in the skillet. Cook for 5 minutes over medium heat or just until the vegetables are tender, stirring occasionally. Add the collard greens and garlic. Cook, covered, for 10 minutes or until tender, stirring occasionally. Remove from the heat. Add the cream cheese, Monterey Jack cheese, cream and Cajun seasoning and mix well. Trim the fatty part from the bacon and discard, if desired. Crumble the remaining bacon and stir into the collard mixture. Spread in a 1 1/2-quart baking dish or 9-inch baking dish. Bake at 350 degrees for 10 minutes or until heated through. Serve with breadsticks or vegetable dippers.

Yield: 3 1/2 cups

Hot Corn Dip

1 cup (2 sticks) butter
16 ounces cream cheese
1/4 cup milk
4 (12-ounce) cans
　Mexicorn, drained
1 (6-ounce) jar pickled
　jalapeño chiles, drained
6 ounces Cheddar cheese,
　shredded

Melt the butter, cream cheese and milk in a saucepan, stirring frequently. Stir in the corn and jalapeño chiles. Fold in the cheese. Pour into a greased 2-quart baking dish. Bake at 315 degrees for 30 minutes. Serve with corn scoops.

Yield: 15 to 20 servings

Feta Black Bean Dip

1/4 cup sugar
3/4 cup apple cider vinegar
3/4 cup vegetable oil
3 (15-ounce) cans black beans, drained and rinsed
3 (15-ounce) cans Shoe Peg corn, drained and rinsed
1 bunch scallions, chopped
1 bunch cilantro, chopped
8 ounces feta cheese, crumbled

Whisk the sugar, vinegar and oil together in a large bowl. Add the black beans, corn, scallions, cilantro and cheese and mix well. Chill until serving time. Serve with tortilla chips or corn chips.

Yield: 3 cups

Grand Marnier Dip

Arrange a variety of fruits (such as fresh pineapple, cantaloupe, honeydew melon, apple chunks, mango, grapes, and strawberries) in a basket or on a platter. If you cut the fruit the day before, especially the pineapple, be sure to marinate it in a sealable plastic bag with orange juice to prevent discoloration. Place the bowl of dip alongside or in the middle of the platter.

8 ounces cream cheese, softened
1/4 cup Grand Marnier, or 2 teaspoons almond extract
2 tablespoons cream
2 tablespoons confectioners' sugar
2 tablespoons chopped almonds, toasted
Fresh strawberries, green grapes, pineapple spears or apple wedges

Beat the cream cheese in a mixing bowl until smooth. Add the Grand Marnier, cream and confectioners' sugar gradually, beating constantly. Stir in the almonds. Spoon into a serving bowl. Chill until serving time. Use as a dip for fresh fruit.

Yield: 1 cup

Feta cheese, the classic Greek cheese, is made of sheep's or goat's milk, although now large commercial producers often make it with cow's milk. It is white, crumbly, and rindless. It makes a great addition for salads.

Caramelized Onion and Mushroom Dip

This takes very little time to make and is always eaten quickly.
Serve with pita chips or Herbed Crostini on page 76.

3 cups chopped sweet onions
  such as Vidalia onions
  (about 2)
2 tablespoons olive oil
3 tablespoons brown sugar
3 tablespoons balsamic
  vinegar
3 tablespoons red wine
1 pound chopped wild or
  domestic mushrooms
16 ounces cream cheese,
  softened
Salt and pepper to taste

Sauté the onions in the olive oil in a skillet.
Add the brown sugar, balsamic vinegar
and red wine. Cook until the onions begin
to caramelize, stirring frequently. Add the
mushrooms. Cook until the mushrooms begin
to soften, stirring frequently. Process the cream
cheese in a food processor until smooth. Add
the onion mixture, salt and pepper. Pulse until
mixed but not puréed. Serve with pita chips.

Yield: 20 servings

*Mulled Cider is so good in
the fall and winter months.
It is great served from a
large pot in the kitchen.
For a more formal
gathering, serve from a
punch bowl or soup tureen.*

Mulled Cider

3 quarts apple cider
1 cup granulated sugar
1 cup packed brown sugar
1 teaspoon ground allspice
1/2 teaspoon ground cloves
4 quarts orange juice
Cinnamon sticks (optional)

Bring the cider, granulated sugar, brown sugar,
allspice and cloves to a boil in a large saucepan.
Boil for 5 minutes. Stir in the orange juice.
Ladle into mugs with cinnamon sticks to serve.

Yield: about 7 quarts

Sparkling Fruit Juice

This refreshing blend of pineapple, orange, and grapefruit juices made effervescent with a sparkling water is a step up from plain juice, but it is just as easy to make. Float a slice or two of a blood orange in the pitcher to dress it up.

1½ cups chilled pineapple
    juice
½ cup chilled orange juice
¼ cup chilled grapefruit
    juice
1 tablespoon lemon juice
1½ cups chilled sparkling
    mineral water
Ice cubes

Blend the pineapple juice, orange juice, grapefruit juice and lemon juice in a pitcher. Stir in the mineral water gradually. Serve over ice.

Yield: four 8-ounce servings

Spiced Iced Tea

2 quarts water
2 (3-inch) cinnamon sticks
½ teaspoon whole cloves
¼ teaspoon nutmeg
3 family-size tea bags
½ cup sugar
1 (6-ounce) can frozen
    orange juice concentrate,
    thawed
1 (6-ounce) can frozen
    lemonade concentrate,
    thawed
Fresh mint leaves (optional)

Bring the water, cinnamon sticks, cloves and nutmeg to a boil in a stockpot. Remove from the heat. Add the tea bags. Steep, covered, for 5 minutes. Discard the tea bags, cinnamon and cloves with a slotted spoon. Stir in the sugar until dissolved. Stir in the orange juice concentrate and lemonade concentrate. Chill until serving time. Serve over ice with fresh mint.

Yield: 2 quarts

Mint Juleps

Every good Southern girl has a recipe for mint juleps. The syrup is no trouble, but you need really good mint leaves.

3 cups fresh mint leaves
2 cups water
2 cups sugar
Juice of 6 limes
Good-quality bourbon
Crushed ice
Fresh mint for garnish

Rinse 3 cups mint thoroughly and place in a pitcher. Bring the water and sugar to a boil in a saucepan, stirring occasionally. Boil for 10 minutes. Pour over the mint. Let steep for several hours. Stir in the lime juice. Strain and pour into a glass jar. Store, tightly sealed, in the refrigerator for several weeks to use as needed. For each mint julep you will need 1 ounce of the mint syrup and 2 ounces bourbon. Mix the syrup and bourbon in a silver julep cup. Add crushed ice and stir until the cup frosts. Garnish with fresh mint.

Yield: enough for 25 servings

Fresh Margaritas

Don't forget to dip the rims of glasses in lemon juice and then in salt. Of course, you can always buy the margarita mix.

4 teaspoons grated lime zest
1/2 cup fresh lime juice
    (from 2 or 3 limes)
4 teaspoons grated
    lemon zest
1/2 cup fresh lemon juice
    (from 2 or 3 lemons)
1/4 cup superfine sugar
Pinch of salt
2 cups crushed ice
1 cup 100 percent tequila
1 cup Triple Sec

Combine the lime zest, lime juice, lemon zest, lemon juice, sugar and salt in a large glass measure. Chill, covered with plastic wrap, for 4 to 24 hours for the flavors to meld. Divide 1 cup of the crushed ice among four to six margarita or double old-fashioned glasses. Strain the juice mixture into a 1-quart pitcher or cocktail shaker. Add the tequila, Triple Sec and remaining 1 cup crushed ice. Stir or shake for 20 to 60 seconds or until thoroughly chilled. Strain into ice-filled glasses and serve immediately.

Yield: 4 to 6 servings

Donna McAnnally, another good cook, gives this suggestion. Bring 4 cups water, 4 cups basil, 2 to 3 cups sugar, and the zest of 1 lemon to a boil in a heavy saucepan. Boil until the sugar is dissolved, stirring occasionally. Remove from the heat and let cool to room temperature. Strain into a glass jar. Add 1 tablespoon to a glass of iced tea for a refreshing drink. Refrigerate the mixture for up to three weeks.

Celebration Punch

*Another good, basic punch recipe. This also can be
served from a punch bowl.*

8 cups cranapple juice
8 cups pineapple juice
1¹/2 cups sugar
2 tablespoons almond extract
2 quarts ginger ale, chilled

Combine the cranapple juice, pineapple juice,
sugar and almond extract in a large pitcher
and mix well. Stir in the ginger ale just before
serving. Serve in a stemmed glass.

Yield: 2¹/2 gallons

Fresh Pineapple and Rum Punch

1 very ripe large pineapple,
   peeled, cored and cut
   into 2-inch pieces
1¹/2 cups water
1¹/4 cups gold rum
¹/4 cup sugar
3 tablespoons fresh lime juice
2 cups 1-inch-cubed fresh
   pineapple
3 cups ice cubes

Combine the very ripe pineapple, water, gold
rum, sugar and lime juice in a large pitcher.
Mash several times with a potato masher. Chill,
covered, for 8 to 10 hours. Strain the mixture
through a coarse sieve set over a large bowl.
Pulse the pineapple solids in a food processor
until coarsely chopped. Strain the chopped
pineapple through a sieve set over the same
bowl, pressing on the solids with a spatula
to release as much liquid as possible. Discard
the pineapple solids in the sieve. Return the
strained pineapple punch to the pitcher. Stir in
2 cups fresh pineapple and the ice cubes before
serving. The punch can be made 6 hours ahead
and stored, covered, in the refrigerator.

Yield: 6 servings

Sunshine Punch

Sometimes we need a punch recipe "in a hurry." This can be used for any occasion—a wedding, tea party, picnic, etc. You also could replace the ginger ale with rum or vodka for a little zip.

3 cups orange juice
3 cups apple juice
3 cups pineapple juice
3 cups chilled ginger ale

Combine the orange juice, apple juice and pineapple juice in a large container and mix well. Chill for 8 to 10 hours for the flavors to meld. Stir in the ginger ale just before serving.

Yield: 3 quarts

John's Rum Punch

Our dear friends, the Lovejoys, hosted us in the Abacos last summer on their yacht. The rum punch, having very few calories, is John's concoction, which we enjoyed thoroughly.

1 package Crystal Light
   lemonade drink mix
1/2 package Crystal Light
   strawberry drink mix
1/2 package Crystal Light
   orange drink mix
2 quarts water
1 quart pineapple juice
2 shakers of bitters
1 (750-milliliter) bottle
   dark rum
1 cup coconut rum
Nutmeg for sprinkling

Combine the drink mixes, water, pineapple juice, bitters, dark rum and coconut rum in a gallon container and mix well. Sprinkle nutmeg over the top.

Yield: 1 gallon

Black Bean Soup

This is quite a nice supper and so tasty served with a green salad and French bread. Puréeing this soup gives it an elegant touch.

2¹/2 cups dried black beans
(about 1 pound)
8 ounces andouille sausage
or Conecuh spicy sausage,
cut into small pieces
1 yellow onion, chopped
3 large garlic cloves, chopped
6 cups water
2 cups chicken broth
1 tablespoon red wine vinegar
1 teaspoon sugar
1¹/2 cups heavy cream
Salt and pepper to taste
1 small red onion, chopped
Sour cream for garnish

Place the beans, sausage, yellow onion, garlic, water, broth, vinegar and sugar in a 4-quart saucepan. Simmer, partially covered, for 2 hours or until the beans are tender. Purée the mixture and return to the saucepan. Stir in the cream, salt and pepper. Ladle into soup bowls. Sprinkle with the red onion. Garnish with a dollop of sour cream.

Yield: eight (1-cup) servings

The Conecuh Sausage Company is located in Greenville, Alabama, and produces the very best smoked sausages. My husband loves it, as it tastes like the sausage his grandparents made on the farm in Brewton, Alabama. Our friend Barney Lovelace brings it to us when he's down that way.

Red Beans and Rice

1 pound red kidney beans,
    drained and rinsed
1 ham hock plus leftover
    ham bits, cut up
2 cups chopped red onion
2 or 3 garlic cloves, minced
2 cups chopped celery
    with leaves
3 quarts water
1 tablespoon salt
1 teaspoon coarsely ground
    black pepper
1 dried red pepper pod, or
    1 teaspoon cayenne pepper
1 pound smoked sausage,
    sliced, sautéed and drained
Fluffy Rice (below)

Bring the beans, ham, onion, garlic, celery, water, salt, black pepper and red pepper to a boil in a large heavy saucepan. Reduce the heat and simmer for 4 to 4½ hours or until the beans are soft and the liquid is thick. Stir in the sausage. Cook for 30 minutes. Adjust the seasonings to taste. Serve over hot Fluffy Rice. Use Conecuh sausage if available.

Yield: 10 to 12 servings

Fluffy Rice

2 cups water
1 cup rice
2 teaspoons salt

Combine the water, rice and salt in a heavy saucepan. Prepare using the package directions. Fluff with a fork after draining. You may cook ahead and reheat before serving.

Yield: 10 to 12 servings

Broccoli Cheese Soup

Do you know anyone who does not love good ol' Broccoli Cheese Soup? You can cut the calories by using nonfat chicken broth, milk instead of cream, and low-fat Cheddar cheese.

1/4 cup (1/2 stick) butter
1 cup chopped onion
1/2 teaspoon minced garlic
3 tablespoons
   all-purpose flour
2 1/2 cups chicken broth
2 cups half-and-half
1 (14-ounce) package frozen
   broccoli florets, cut into
   small pieces
3/4 teaspoon salt
1/4 teaspoon white pepper
1/8 teaspoon dried thyme
2 cups (8 ounces) shredded
   Cheddar cheese
Fresh thyme for garnish

Melt the butter in a large heavy saucepan over medium heat. Add the onion and cook for 5 minutes. Add the garlic and cook for 3 minutes. Stir in the flour. Cook for 2 minutes, stirring constantly. Whisk in the broth and half-and-half. Stir in the broccoli, salt, white pepper and dried thyme. Bring to a boil. Reduce the heat and simmer, uncovered, for 20 minutes. Add the cheese. Heat until melted and smooth, stirring constantly. Ladle into soup bowls. Garnish with fresh thyme. Serve immediately.

Yield: four (1-cup) servings

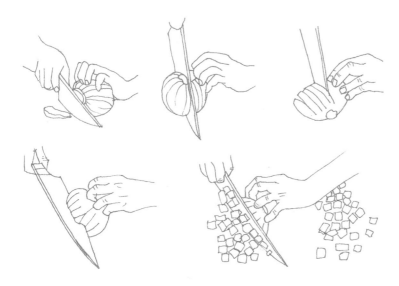

Moroccan Carrot Soup

Great flavor! The carrots are said to make your eyesight more keen.

2 tablespoons butter
1 cup chopped white onion
1 pound large carrots, cut
    into 1/2-inch pieces
    (about 2 1/2 cups)
2 1/2 cups low-sodium
    chicken broth
1 tablespoon honey
1 1/2 teaspoons chili powder
1 teaspoon fresh lemon juice
1/8 teaspoon ground allspice
Salt and pepper to taste
1/2 cup plain yogurt, stirred
Ground cumin for sprinkling

Melt the butter in a large saucepan over medium-high heat. Add the onion and sauté for 2 minutes. Stir in the carrots. Add the broth and bring to a boil. Reduce the heat. Simmer, covered, for 20 minutes or until the carrots are very tender. Remove from the heat. Purée in batches in a blender and return to the saucepan. Whisk in the honey, chili powder, lemon juice and allspice. Sprinkle with salt and pepper. Ladle into soup bowls. Drizzle with the yogurt. Sprinkle generously with cumin.

Yield: 4 servings

Loaded Potato Soup

Always tasty and filling.

6 slices bacon
1/2 cup chopped green onions
1 (14-ounce) can
    vegetable broth
1 1/2 pounds red potatoes,
    cut into cubes
1 cup sour cream
1 cup milk
1 teaspoon kosher salt
1 teaspoon freshly
    ground pepper
Shredded Cheddar cheese
    and chopped fresh chives
    for topping

Cook the bacon in a large heavy saucepan until crisp. Remove the bacon to paper towels to drain. Crumble the bacon when cool. Drain the saucepan, reserving 1 tablespoon of the drippings in the saucepan. Add the green onions. Sauté over medium-high heat for 3 minutes or until tender. Add the broth and potatoes. Cook until tender. Whisk in the sour cream and milk. Add the salt and pepper. Cook for 15 minutes or until heated through. Ladle into soup bowls. Top with the bacon, cheese and chives.

Yield: 6 servings

Comfort Soup

My sweet friend, Barbara Baugh, brought many people comfort with this special soup. To be so easy, it is extra special and soothing. Just the ticket for a sick friend or a quick dinner on a cold night.

1 (5-ounce) package
    au gratin potatoes
3 cups water
1 (10-ounce) can tomatoes
    with green chiles
1 (16-ounce) can whole
    kernel corn, drained
2 cups milk
2 cups cubed Velveeta cheese

Combine the potatoes with sauce mix, water, tomatoes with green chiles, and corn in a large saucepan and mix well. Cook until the potatoes are tender. Add the milk and cheese. Heat until the cheese melts, stirring constantly. Ladle into soup bowls.

Yield: 4 to 6 servings

Butternut Squash Soup

A very special fall and winter soup. It is so appealing served in a hollowed-out pumpkin at Thanksgiving.

2 large butternut squash, cut into halves and seeded
2 tablespoons butter
2 tablespoons olive oil
1 cup chopped onion
1 cup chopped carrot
1 tablespoon minced garlic
1 teaspoon ground coriander
2 quarts chicken broth
1 teaspoon pepper
1 teaspoon sugar
1 1/2 cups (6 ounces) freshly grated Parmesan cheese
1/2 cup heavy whipping cream
3 tablespoons dry sherry
Pumpernickel croutons for garnish

Place the squash cut side down on a lightly greased baking sheet and pierce several times with a fork. Bake at 375 degrees for 1 hour or until tender. Let cool slightly before handling. Scrape out the cooked squash into a bowl with a large spoon, discarding the shell, and set aside. Heat the butter and olive oil in a stockpot over medium heat until the butter melts. Add the onion, carrot, garlic and coriander. Cook for 10 to 12 minutes or until tender, stirring frequently. Add the squash, broth, pepper and sugar and mix well. Reduce the heat to medium-low. Simmer, covered, for 45 minutes. Remove from the heat to cool slightly. Purée the squash mixture in batches until smooth. Return the squash mixture to the stockpot. Add the cheese, cream and sherry. Cook over medium-low heat for 5 minutes or until the cheese melts, stirring constantly. Ladle into soup bowls. Garnish with pumpernickel croutons.

Yield: 4 quarts

Chicken and Wild Rice Soup

*If I had to pick a soup that I think is absolutely divine,
I would pick this one. My great friend, Eydie Swanson, sends me wild
rice from Minnesota, but it's easy to find in the South.*

3 (14-ounce) cans
   chicken broth
1 cup chopped carrot
1/2 cup wild rice, rinsed
   and drained
1/2 cup chopped celery
1/2 cup chopped onion
2 cups sliced mushrooms
2 tablespoons butter or
   margarine
1/4 cup all-purpose flour
1/4 teaspoon salt
1/4 teaspoon pepper
1 cup whipping cream
2 cups chopped cooked
   chicken (10 ounces)
Chopped chives for garnish

Combine 2 cans of the broth, the carrot, wild rice, celery and onion in a 4-quart stockpot. Bring to a boil. Reduce the heat and simmer, covered, for 35 to 40 minutes or until the wild rice is tender but still chewy, adding the mushrooms during the last 5 minutes. Melt the butter over medium heat in a saucepan. Stir in the flour, salt and pepper. Add the remaining 1 can broth. Cook until thickened and bubbly, stirring constantly. Cook for 1 minute longer, stirring constantly. Stir in the cream. Add to the wild rice mixture, stirring constantly. Stir in the chicken. Cook until heated through. Ladle into soup bowls. Garnish with chopped chives. Serve with toasted baguette slices.

Yield: 8 servings

Shrimp and Crab Gumbo

This can be doubled for a large group. I love using aromatic basmati rice.

1/2 cup canola oil
1/2 cup all-purpose flour
4 quarts water
2 onions, finely chopped
1 large bell pepper,
    finely chopped
4 ribs celery, finely chopped
4 (16-ounce) cans sliced okra
1 (16-ounce) can
    diced tomatoes
2 tablespoons
    Worcestershire sauce
2 garlic cloves, minced
1 to 2 teaspoons cayenne
    pepper
2 pounds shrimp, peeled
    and deveined
1 pound white crab meat,
    shells removed and flaked
2 tablespoons gumbo
    filé powder
Salt and black pepper
    to taste
Hot steamed white rice

Heat the canola oil in a medium saucepan or skillet over medium heat. Add the flour and mix well. Reduce the heat to low. Cook until the roux turns medium brown in color, stirring constantly. The roux can be made ahead and stored in the refrigerator until ready to use. Bring the water to a boil in a large stockpot over medium-high heat. Add the roux and cook until dissolved. Add the onions and cook until translucent. Add the bell pepper and celery and cook for a few minutes. Add the okra, tomatoes, Worcestershire sauce, garlic and cayenne pepper and return to a boil. Reduce the heat to low. Simmer for 2 hours. Add the shrimp, crab meat and gumbo filé powder. Cook for 30 minutes. Sprinkle with salt and black pepper. Ladle over rice in soup bowls.

Yield: 12 to 15 servings

The Sebastian Sandwich

Years ago my friend, Katherine Wilks, and I hosted a casual picnic supper at the river. I think we made a hundred of these sandwiches, and our guests really enjoyed them. We served hot German potato salad (or any potato salad could be served) and three-bean baked beans, plus cake squares for dessert.

2/3 cup mayonnaise
1/3 cup chopped
   mango chutney
1 tablespoon curry powder
1 teaspoon salt
3 cups medium
   shredded cabbage
12 slices rye bread
6 (1-ounce) slices
   Cheddar cheese
6 thin slices cooked
   smoked ham

Mix the mayonnaise, chutney, curry powder and salt in a bowl. Add the cabbage and toss to coat. Spoon about 1/4 cup of the cabbage mixture on each of six slices of rye bread. Stack a cheese slice and ham slice on top of each. Top with the remaining slices of rye bread. Cut the sandwiches into halves. Wrap each sandwich in foil and place on a baking sheet. Bake at 350 degrees until the cheese melts.

Yield: 6 sandwiches

Easiest Pimento Cheese

This is truly a tasty pimento cheese with a bit of "zing." My friend, Pat Hoover, sends this from Atlanta and states you may substitute light mayonnaise and cheeses for a less caloric version.

1/2 cup mayonnaise
1/2 cup sour cream
4 ounces cream cheese,
   softened
16 ounces sharp Cheddar
   cheese, shredded
8 ounces Pepper Jack cheese,
   shredded (optional)
1 (4-ounce) jar chopped
   pimentos, drained
1/2 teaspoon freshly
   ground pepper
Salt to taste

Combine the mayonnaise, sour cream, cream cheese, Cheddar cheese, Pepper Jack cheese, pimentos, pepper and salt in a medium bowl and mix well. Add more or less mayonnaise for the desired consistency. Chill, covered, until serving time.

Yield: about 3 cups

Betty's Pimento Cheese

3 cups (12 ounces)
   shredded sharp
   Cheddar cheese
1 1/2 cups (6 ounces)
   shredded Swiss cheese
2 (4-ounce) jars pimentos,
   chopped and drained
2 cups mayonnaise
2 teaspoons garlic salt
2 teaspoons dried
   dill weed

Combine the Cheddar cheese, Swiss cheese, pimentos, mayonnaise, garlic salt and dill weed in a bowl and mix well. Chill, covered, until serving time.

Yield: 4 1/2 cups

Salmon BLTs with Lemon-Dill Sauce

*I dearly love salmon, and this sandwich is one you
can serve to weekend guests or your family.*

1/3 cup light mayonnaise
2 teaspoons chopped fresh
   dill weed
1 teaspoon grated fresh
   lemon zest
4 (6-ounce) pieces salmon
   fillets with skin,
   1 inch thick
1/4 teaspoon salt
1/8 teaspoon coarsely
   ground pepper
8 (1/2-inch-thick) center
   slices country-style bread
   or ciabatta
8 romaine lettuce leaves
2 tomatoes, sliced
6 slices bacon, fully cooked
   and cut into halves

Mix the mayonnaise, dill weed and lemon zest in a small bowl and set aside. Sprinkle the salmon with the salt and pepper. Place salmon skin side down on a lightly greased grill rack. Grill, covered, over medium heat for 10 to 12 minutes or until the salmon is opaque throughout and begins to flake. Do not turn. Slide a metal spatula between the salmon flesh and skin. Lift the salmon from the skin and place on a plate, discarding the skin, if desired. Place the bread on the grill rack. Grill for 1 minute on each side or until lightly toasted. Spread the lemon-dill mayonnaise on one side of the bread slices. Place two lettuce leaves on each of four bread slices. Top each with the salmon, tomatoes and bacon. Top with the remaining bread slices.

Yield: 4 servings

Baked Pears with Walnuts over Mixed Greens

If you buy ready-to-use bagged greens, they are not really safe to eat until you wash them. Please beware.

4 large pears, peeled
1/2 cup sugar
1/2 cup water
1 teaspoon cinnamon
2 cups walnuts
1/2 cup (1 stick) unsalted butter, cut into 1-inch slices
2 (5-ounce) packages mixed greens, rinsed and dried

Cut the pears into quarters and place in a greased 2-quart baking dish. Sprinkle with the sugar. Add the water, cinnamon, walnuts and butter. Bake, covered, at 350 degrees for 45 minutes. Remove from the oven to cool. Serve over the mixed greens. Use Betty's Simple Vinaigrette (page 123) to dress the mixed greens before placing the pears over the greens.

Yield: 8 servings

Spinach Salad with Mango-Ginger Chutney Dressing

1 cup pecans
2 bunches small-leaf spinach, trimmed, rinsed and drained
2 apples, cut into halves crosswise and thinly sliced
1/2 to 3/4 cup raisins
1/2 cup chopped green onions
Mango-Ginger Chutney Dressing (at right)

Spread the pecans in a single layer on a baking sheet. Bake at 200 degrees for 30 to 40 minutes or until toasted. Let cool on a wire rack. Combine the spinach, apples, toasted pecans, raisins and green onions in a large bowl. Add the dressing and toss to coat. Serve immediately.

Yield: 8 to 10 servings

Mango-Ginger Chutney Dressing

1 teaspoon curry powder
1 teaspoon dry mustard
1/2 teaspoon salt
2 tablespoons fresh lemon juice
1 teaspoon sugar
1/2 cup canola oil
1/4 cup mango-ginger chutney

Combine the curry powder, dry mustard, salt, lemon juice and sugar in a small bowl and mix well. Whisk in the canola oil in a slow steady stream until thick or emulsified. Stir in the chutney.

Yield: about 1 cup

Cherry, Blue Cheese and Pine Nut Salad

Janet Jenkins, my dear friend who hails from the North and who now has become a real Southerner, brings this recipe from her home in Traverse City, Michigan. Did you know that Michigan is the number one cherry-producing state in the country? Maple syrup really "makes" the dressing.

1/2 cup raspberry vinegar
1/2 cup olive oil
1/2 cup vegetable oil
1/2 cup maple syrup
2 tablespoons Dijon mustard
2 tablespoons fresh
    tarragon leaves
1/2 teaspoon salt
3 heads red leaf lettuce,
    rinsed and torn
1/4 cup crumbled blue cheese
12 red onion rings
Dried cherries to taste
1 tablespoon pine nuts,
    pecans or walnuts,
    lightly sautéed

Combine the vinegar, olive oil, vegetable oil, maple syrup, Dijon mustard, tarragon and salt in a small bowl and mix well. Place the lettuce in a large salad bowl. Add 3/4 cup of the dressing and toss by hand. Top with the blue cheese, onion rings, dried cherries and pine nuts. Serve the remaining dressing on the side.

Yield: 10 servings

Iceberg Lettuce Wedge with Blue Cheese Dressing

For years this was such a popular salad, and now it's back! Use all ingredients "full blast," not low fat, if you prefer. Iceberg lettuce has roughage but very few nutrients—much less than romaine lettuce or leaf lettuce.

8 slices thick-cut bacon
2 heads iceberg lettuce
1 cup chopped tomato
4 hard-cooked eggs, chopped
Blue cheese crumbles
   for garnish
Blue Cheese Dressing
   (at right)

Fry the bacon in a skillet until crisp. Remove the bacon to paper towels to drain. Crumble the bacon and set aside. Cut the lettuce into quarters and remove the core. Place each wedge on an individual serving plate or a platter. Top each with the bacon, tomato and chopped eggs. Garnish with the cheese. Add Blue Cheese Dressing and serve.

Yield: 8 servings

Blue Cheese Dressing

8 ounces reduced-fat
   cream cheese
1/2 cup reduced-fat
   mayonnaise
1/2 cup (2 ounces)
   crumbled blue cheese
1 teaspoon
   Worcestershire sauce
2 tablespoons
   low-fat milk
1/8 teaspoon pepper

Process the cream cheese, mayonnaise, blue cheese, Worcestershire sauce, milk and pepper in a food processor to break up any large pieces of the blue cheese. Serve immediately or chill in an airtight container for up to one week.

Yield: 8 servings

Asian Coleslaw

A bit different from conventional slaw—so good.

5 cups Chinese cabbage,
   coarsely chopped
1 cup shredded carrots
1/2 cup julienned
   green onions
1 (8-ounce) can sliced water
   chestnuts, drained
2 tablespoons sesame
   seeds, toasted
1/2 cup vegetable oil
1 teaspoon dark sesame oil
2 tablespoons sugar
1 tablespoon minced cilantro
1/2 teaspoon pepper
1/2 cup wine vinegar
1 tablespoon soy sauce

Combine the cabbage, carrots, green onions, water chestnuts and sesame seeds in a bowl and toss well. Whisk the vegetable oil, sesame oil, sugar, cilantro, pepper, vinegar and soy sauce together in a bowl. Pour over the vegetables and toss to coat. Chill, covered, for 2 hours. Toss again before serving.

Yield: 12 servings

Layered Taco Salad

2 ripe avocados
1/2 cup minced cilantro
1/2 cup mayonnaise
1/4 cup buttermilk
2 tablespoons fresh lime juice
2 teaspoons hot pepper sauce
1/2 teaspoon sugar
1/4 teaspoon salt
1 (10-ounce) package hearts
   of romaine lettuce, torn
2 cups chopped cooked
   chicken
2 cups sour cream
1 (15-ounce) can chili
   beans, drained
1 (15-ounce) can yellow corn
   kernels, drained
1 (15-ounce) can black
   beans, drained and rinsed
1 (14-ounce) can diced fire-
   roasted tomatoes, drained
2 cups (8 ounces) shredded
   Mexican cheese blend
1/2 cup minced green onions
Crushed tortilla chips
   for garnish

Process the avocados, cilantro, mayonnaise, buttermilk, lime juice, hot sauce, sugar and salt in a food processor until smooth. Chill, covered, for up to 8 hours. Layer the lettuce, chicken, sour cream, chili beans, corn, black beans, tomatoes, cheese and green onions in a large serving bowl. Spread the avocado dressing evenly over the top layer. Chill, covered, for up to 8 hours before serving. Garnish with tortilla chips.

Yield: 8 to 10 servings

Avocados are extremely low in carbohydrates—less than three grams in a typical serving (one-fifth of an avocado)—most of it fiber. Their mono- and poly-unsaturated fats are not only recommended for heart health, but also give a feeling of satiety, or fullness, that helps people stick to a weight-loss diet. Avocados also are approved for diabetic diets. There are endless ways to enjoy these benefits, from using seasoned avocado as a nutrient-dense spread to spooning a zingy avocado salsa over steak or fish.

Watermelon Cucumber Salad with Mint Vinaigrette

How refreshing! It is, of course, limited to the summer months when watermelons are plentiful.

1/4 cup rice vinegar
2 tablespoons sugar
2 tablespoons chopped
   fresh mint
1/2 teaspoon red pepper
   flakes
2 cups chopped seedless
   watermelon
2 cups thinly sliced
   seeded cucumbers
1/2 cup thinly sliced
   red onion

Whisk the vinegar, sugar, mint and pepper flakes together in a large bowl until the sugar dissolves. Add the watermelon, cucumbers and onion and toss to coat. Chill, covered, until serving time.

Yield: 4 1/2 cups

Betty's Simple Vinaigrette

By using olive oil, it is very healthy and a cinch to whisk up in a hurry.

3 tablespoons fresh
   lemon juice
3 tablespoons honey
1 cup extra-virgin olive oil
1 teaspoon salt
1/2 teaspoon freshly
   ground pepper

Whisk the lemon juice and honey together in a small bowl. Add the olive oil gradually, whisking until the vinaigrette is emulsified or thick. Whisk in the salt and pepper. Store in the refrigerator for up to 3 weeks.

Yield: 1 1/4 cups

Power Foods

Power foods offer a big nutritional bang for their calorie buck.

Almonds
Bell peppers
Blueberries
Broccoli
Olive oil
Grapes
Spinach
Strawberries
Tomatoes
Whole grains

French Vinaigrette

Great for French potato salad.

1/2 cup Dijon mustard
2 tablespoons plus
   2 teaspoons dry mustard
2 tablespoons plus
   2 teaspoons salt
Cracked pepper to taste
8 garlic cloves, minced
1 cup tarragon vinegar
1/2 cup lemon juice
2 cups olive oil
2 cups canola oil

Whisk the Dijon mustard, dry mustard, salt, pepper, garlic, vinegar and lemon juice together in a bowl. Add the olive oil and canola oil gradually, whisking constantly until emulsified.

Yield: 1 1/2 quarts

French Dressing

2 cups ketchup
2 cups sugar
1 cup apple cider vinegar
1 cup canola oil
1 onion, cut into chunks

Process the ketchup, sugar, vinegar, canola oil and onion in a blender or food processor until smooth.

Yield: 1 1/2 quarts

Vidalia Onion Pie

3 cups thinly sliced
   Vidalia onions
3 tablespoons unsalted
   butter, melted
1 baked (10-inch) deep-dish
   pie shell
1/2 cup milk
1 1/2 cups sour cream
1 teaspoon salt
2 eggs, beaten
3 tablespoons
   all-purpose flour
4 slices bacon, crisp-fried
   and crumbled

Sauté the onions in the butter in a skillet until light brown. Spoon into the pie shell. Combine the milk, sour cream, salt, eggs and flour in a bowl and mix well. Pour over the onion mixture. Sprinkle with the bacon. Bake at 325 degrees for 30 minutes or until firm in the center.

Yield: 6 to 8 servings

Mushroom, Spinach and Cheese Frittata

Scrambled eggs with cheese is always a winner. This could be assembled the day before, covered, and chilled. Remove from the refrigerator an hour before baking. Top with the tomatoes and Parmesan cheese just before baking.

3 tablespoons unsalted butter
1 pint sliced wild or
 domestic mushrooms
3 tablespoons chopped onion
1 (10-ounce) package frozen
 chopped spinach, thawed
 and squeezed dry
Salt to taste
1 cup (4 ounces) shredded
 Cheddar cheese
1/2 cup (2 ounces) shredded
 Swiss cheese
1 cup sour cream
2 tablespoons chopped chives
8 eggs
3 tablespoons heavy cream
2 tablespoons unsalted butter
Pepper to taste
2 tomatoes, peeled and sliced
2 tablespoons grated
 Parmesan cheese

Melt 3 tablespoons butter in a medium skillet. Add the mushrooms, onion and spinach. Sauté for 3 minutes. Sprinkle lightly with salt. Place in a greased quiche dish or 9×9-inch baking pan. Sprinkle with one-half of the Cheddar cheese and one-half of the Swiss cheese. Spread with the sour cream and chives. Beat the eggs with the cream in a bowl. Melt 2 tablespoons butter in a medium skillet. Add the egg mixture. Cook until softly scrambled, stirring frequently. Sprinkle with salt and pepper. Spread over the chives. Sprinkle with the remaining Cheddar cheese and Swiss cheese. Arrange the tomatoes over the top. Sprinkle with the Parmesan cheese. Bake at 400 degrees for 35 minutes.

Yield: 8 to 10 servings

Tropical Ambrosia

My sweet mother always made the ambrosia for the holidays when I was growing up and until she no longer could cook. Hers was delicious and, of course, we used the seedless navel oranges. See page 127 for another version.

14 navel oranges, sectioned
1 pineapple, chopped
1 cup chopped pecans
1 1/2 cups frozen flaked coconut or freshly grated coconut

Combine the oranges and pineapple in a large bowl and mix well. Chill, covered, until serving time. Stir in the pecans and coconut just before serving.

Yield: 8 to 10 servings

Fancy Egg Scramble

Marie Thomas, a super cook and hostess, serves this and receives rave reviews. A brunch dish, this can be made ahead.

1 cup (4 ounces) finely chopped baked ham
1/4 cup chopped green onions
3 tablespoons butter
12 eggs, beaten
1 (3-ounce) can mushroom stems and pieces, drained
Cheese Sauce (below)
1/4 cup (1/2 stick) butter, melted
2 1/4 cups soft bread crumbs (about 3 bread slices)
1/8 teaspoon paprika

Sauté the ham and green onions in 3 tablespoons butter in a large skillet over medium heat until the green onions are tender. Add the eggs and cook just until set, stirring frequently. Combine the mushrooms, egg mixture and Cheese Sauce in a bowl and stir gently. Spoon into a 9×12-inch baking dish. Combine 1/4 cup butter with the bread crumbs and paprika in a bowl and mix well. Sprinkle over the egg mixture. Chill, covered, for 1 hour. Bake at 350 degrees for 30 minutes.

Yield: 6 servings

Cheese Sauce

2 tablespoons butter
2 tablespoons all-purpose flour
1/2 teaspoon salt
1/8 teaspoon pepper
2 cups milk
1 cup (4 ounces) shredded sharp Cheddar cheese

Melt the butter in a saucepan over medium heat. Stir in the flour, salt and pepper. Add the milk. Cook until bubbly and thickened, stirring constantly. Add the cheese and heat until melted, stirring constantly.

Tomato Florentine Quiche

If you do not have Italian bread crumbs on hand, just add plain bread crumbs and a teaspoon of dried basil and a teaspoon of dried oregano. Use 4 teaspoons of fresh herbs.

1 (10-ounce) package frozen
  chopped spinach, thawed
1 (14-ounce) can petite diced
  tomatoes, drained
2 tablespoons Italian
  bread crumbs
3 eggs, lightly beaten
1 cup half-and-half
4 slices bacon, cooked
  and crumbled
1/2 cup (2 ounces) shredded
  sharp Cheddar cheese
1/2 cup (2 ounces) shredded
  mozzarella cheese
1 teaspoon dried basil
1/4 teaspoon ground
  red pepper
1 unbaked (10-inch) deep-
  dish pie shell
Sprigs of Italian parsley
  for garnish

Drain the spinach in a wire-mesh strainer, pressing with several paper towels to remove the excess water. Toss the tomatoes with the bread crumbs in a bowl. Combine the spinach, eggs, half-and-half, bacon, Cheddar cheese, mozzarella cheese, basil and red pepper in a large bowl and mix well. Fold in the tomato mixture. Spoon into the pie shell and place on a baking sheet. Bake at 350 degrees for 50 to 60 minutes or until set. Remove from the oven. Let stand for 20 minutes before serving. Garnish with Italian parsley.

Yield: 6 to 8 servings

Ambrosia

1 cup drained
  pineapple chunks
1 cup drained
  mandarin oranges
1 cup grated coconut
1 cup chopped pecans
1 cup sour cream
  (optional)

Combine the pineapple, mandarin oranges, coconut, pecans and sour cream in a bowl and mix well. Chill, covered, until serving time.

Yield: 5 cups

Braised Apples

2 tablespoons
    brown sugar
2 tablespoons maple syrup
2 tablespoons honey
4 Fuji apples, cut into
    wedges
1 teaspoon ground
    cinnamon
1 cup fruity red wine,
    such as pinot noir

Combine the brown sugar, maple syrup and honey in a large nonstick skillet and mix well. Stir in the apples. Cook over medium-high heat until the apples are nearly cooked through, stirring frequently. Add the cinnamon. Stir in the wine. Cook for 3 minutes or until the apples are tender and the liquid is slightly reduced, stirring frequently.

Yield: 6 servings

Delicious Bacon Brunch Casserole

A great friendship began when Katherine Wilks and I spent time together planning, testing, and organizing Cotton Country Cooking. She uses this hearty brunch casserole for her "always-hungry" University of Alabama football stars when they visit her. These guys are the sons of Karen and Glenn Love of Birmingham. Kathy Littrell and Karen Love, Katherine's daughters, plus son, John, are all good cooks.

1/2 cup (1 stick) unsalted
    butter, melted
4 tomatoes, sliced
1 large red bell pepper,
    cut into strips
8 ounces mushrooms, sliced
2 cups (8 ounces) shredded
    Cheddar cheese
1 pound bacon, cooked
    and crumbled
16 eggs, beaten
2 tablespoons water
1 teaspoon dry mustard
1 teaspoon salt
1/2 teaspoon pepper

Pour the butter into a 3-quart rectangular baking dish. Layer the tomatoes, bell pepper, mushrooms, cheese and bacon over the butter. Beat the eggs, water, dry mustard, salt and pepper in a bowl. Pour over the layers. Bake at 350 degrees for 45 minutes.

Yield: 6 servings

Brunch Chicken Sandwich

This is one of my all-time favorites to serve for brunch or lunch. Served with Copper Penny Carrots (at right) and marinated asparagus, it makes a yummy meal.

2 cups chopped cooked
   chicken
1 cup (4 ounces) shredded
   Cheddar cheese
1/2 cup mayonnaise
12 slices white bread,
   trimmed
6 eggs
3 cups milk
3/4 to 1 teaspoon salt
1 cup sliced almonds

Mix the chicken, cheese and mayonnaise in a bowl. Spread on one-half of the bread slices. Top with the remaining bread slices. Place in a 9×13-inch baking dish. Beat the eggs, milk and salt in a bowl until smooth. Pour over the sandwiches. Chill, covered, for 8 to 10 hours. Bake, covered, at 350 degrees for 35 minutes. Bake, uncovered, for 15 minutes longer.

Yield: 6 servings

Basic Crepes

Crepes take a bit of practice. A great idea is to sprinkle cinnamon-sugar on them and roll them up to be devoured. They are also delicious stuffed with chocolate hazelnut spread and served with a dollop of whipped cream on top.

4 eggs
2 cups unbleached
   all-purpose flour
1 cup (or more) milk
1 cup water
1/4 cup (1/2 stick) butter,
   melted
Pinch of salt
Vegetable oil for brushing

Whisk the eggs and flour together in a bowl. Add 1 cup milk and the water gradually, beating constantly. Beat in the butter and salt. Let rest, covered, in a cool place or chill for 1 hour or longer. Add enough additional milk to the batter to make the desired consistency. Heat a crepe pan over medium heat until a drop of water sizzles on contact. Brush lightly with oil and lift pan off of the heat. Ladle 2 tablespoons of the batter into the skillet, tilting to coat evenly. Cook for 1 minute or until the edge begins to curl from the pan. Turn and cook for 30 seconds. Slide onto a plate. Repeat with the remaining batter, brushing the pan with oil as needed. Stack the crepes between sheets of waxed paper as they are cooked.

Yield: 20 crepes

Copper Penny Carrots

2 pounds carrots, sliced
1 small bell pepper, sliced
1 onion, sliced
1 (10-ounce) can
   tomato soup
1/2 cup vegetable oil
1 cup sugar
3/4 cup vinegar
1 teaspoon mustard
1 teaspoon Worcestershire
   sauce
Salt to taste

Boil the carrots in water in a saucepan until tender and drain. Layer the carrots, bell pepper and onion in an airtight container. Combine the soup, oil, sugar, vinegar, mustard, Worcestershire sauce and salt in a bowl and mix well. Pour over the layered vegetables. Chill, covered, for up to two weeks.

Yield: 16 servings

Mascarpone, Ham and Asparagus Tart

Mascarpone cheese is an Italian creamy cheese. If you prefer
a homemade crust, try the recipe for Perfect Pie Pastry on page 172.

1 refrigerator pie pastry
1 1/2 cups mascarpone cheese
2 tablespoons chopped fresh
    tarragon
4 teaspoons coarse-grain
    mustard
4 teaspoons prepared
    horseradish
Salt and pepper to taste
1 pound asparagus, trimmed
5 cups arugula
8 ounces thinly sliced ham,
    cut into thin strips
1 tablespoon lemon juice
1 teaspoon lemon zest

Fit the pastry into a 10-inch tart pan. Bake at 425 degrees for 12 minutes or until golden brown. Mix the cheese, tarragon, mustard, horseradish, salt and pepper in a bowl. Cut each asparagus spear into four or five pieces. Boil in salted water in a large saucepan for 3 minutes and drain. Plunge immediately into a bowl of ice water to stop the cooking process. Drain well. Toss the asparagus with the arugula, ham, lemon juice, lemon zest and salt and pepper to taste in a medium bowl. Place in the tart shell. Cover with the cheese mixture. Bake for 20 to 30 minutes or until cheese is melted.

Yield: 6 to 8 servings

Pumpkin Shell Casserole

My longtime friend, Liz Pilgrim, who is a super cook and from Georgia, my
home state, gave me this recipe. How pretty at Thanksgiving or any fall brunch!

1 (7- to 8-inch) pumpkin
2 cups chopped peeled apples
1 cup raisins
1 cup packed brown sugar
1 teaspoon lemon juice
1/4 teaspoon ground
    cinnamon
1/4 teaspoon ground nutmeg
1 cup sour cream

Cut a lid from the pumpkin and set aside. Remove the seeds from the pumpkin and discard. Rinse the pumpkin and pat dry. Mix the apples, raisins, brown sugar, lemon juice, cinnamon and nutmeg in a bowl. Spoon into the pumpkin shell and replace the lid. Place on a baking sheet. Bake at 350 degrees for 1 hour or until the apples are tender, wrapping with foil if the pumpkin begins to brown. Serve hot or cold from the shell, being sure to include some of the pumpkin. Top each serving with a dollop of the sour cream.

Yield: 4 to 6 servings

Poached Fruit with Spiced Cream

This recipe is a great addition to any brunch or lunch.

2¹/2 cups apple juice
2 tablespoons mulling
  spice blend
1 pear, chopped
1 cup chopped mango
  or papaya
1 cup sliced apple
¹/3 cup dried cranberries or
  dried cherries
Spiced Cream (below)
Freshly grated nutmeg

Place the apple juice in a medium saucepan. Place the mulling spice blend in the center of a 5-inch double-thick square of one hundred percent cheesecloth. Bring up the corners of the cheesecloth and tie with kitchen string. Add the spice bag to the apple juice. Bring to a boil. Stir in the pear, mango, apple and cranberries. Return to a boil. Reduce the heat and simmer, covered, for 10 minutes or until the fruit is tender. Drain the fruit, reserving the cooking liquid for use in the Spiced Cream. Let the fruit cool slightly. Divide the fruit among six dessert dishes. Serve warm topped with Spiced Cream. Sprinkle each serving with nutmeg.

Yield: 6 servings

Spiced Cream

3 ounces cream cheese,
  softened
¹/4 cup sour cream
¹/4 cup whipping cream
¹/4 cup sifted confectioners'
  sugar
1 to 2 tablespoons reserved
  cooking liquid from
  Poached Fruit (above)

Combine the cream cheese, sour cream, whipping cream and confectioners' sugar in a small bowl and mix well. Add enough of the reserved cooking liquid from the Poached Fruit to make the desired consistency.

Yield: about 1 cup

Nutmeg

Whole nutmeg grated or ground with a grinder is superior to that which is commercially ground and packaged.

Overnight Oven-Baked French Toast

1 (16-ounce) loaf
  French bread
1/4 cup (1/2 stick) unsalted
  butter, softened
4 eggs
1 cup milk
1/4 cup sugar
3 tablespoons maple syrup
1 teaspoon vanilla extract
1/2 teaspoon salt

Cut the bread into ten slices 3/4 inch thick. Spread the butter evenly over one side of each bread slice. Arrange buttered side up in an ungreased 9×12-inch dish. Whisk the eggs, milk, sugar, maple syrup, vanilla and salt in a bowl. Pour over the bread, pressing the slices down. Chill, covered, for 8 hours. Remove the bread slices from the dish and place on two lightly greased baking sheets. Bake, uncovered, at 350 degrees for 45 minutes or until golden brown.

Yield: 8 to 10 servings

Pineapple-Pecan Bread

*Jackie Guice, cookbook author, and I have known each other
for many years—since college to be exact. We traveled together to study
in France. She is so delightful and a great cook.*

2 cups all-purpose flour
1 teaspoon baking soda
1/2 teaspoon salt
3/4 cup packed brown sugar
1/4 cup (1/2 stick) margarine
1 egg
1/3 cup thawed frozen orange
  juice concentrate
1 cup crushed pineapple
1/2 cup chopped pecans

Combine the flour, baking soda and salt in a bowl. Cream the brown sugar and margarine in a large bowl. Beat in the egg. Add the flour mixture alternately with the orange juice concentrate, mixing well after each addition. Stir in the undrained pineapple and the pecans. Pour into a greased 5×9-inch loaf pan. Bake at 350 degrees for 50 to 60 minutes or until the bread tests done.

Yield: 1 loaf

Bran Muffins

Can you imagine any batter lasting two weeks so that you can have fresh muffins at anytime? I love to add 2 teaspoons each of ground cinnamon and ginger to the batter.

1 (15-ounce) package
   Raisin Bran
3 cups sugar
5 cups all-purpose flour
5 teaspoons baking soda
1 teaspoon salt
4 eggs, beaten
1 cup vegetable oil
1 quart buttermilk

Mix the cereal, sugar, flour, baking soda and salt in a large bowl. Add the eggs, oil and buttermilk and mix well. Store, tightly covered, in the refrigerator for up to 2 weeks. To bake, fill greased muffin cups two-thirds full. Bake at 400 degrees for 15 minutes or until the muffins test done. You may bake all the muffins and store in a freezer bag in the freezer. Reheat when needed. To reheat, wrap in foil and bake at 350 degrees until heated through.

Yield: 5 dozen

Chocolate Hazelnut Muffins

Delicious and so easy, you could use these as a dessert as well.

1/2 cup (1 stick) butter
1 ounce unsweetened
   chocolate, finely chopped
1 cup sugar
1/4 cup baking cocoa
2 eggs
1 teaspoon vanilla extract
1/2 teaspoon salt
3/4 cup all-purpose flour
3/4 cup chocolate hazelnut
   spread (Nutella)

Place the butter in a microwave-safe bowl. Microwave on High at 30-second intervals until melted. Stir in the chocolate until smooth. Stir in the sugar and baking cocoa. Whisk in the eggs, vanilla and salt. Stir in the flour until smooth. Spoon evenly into twelve buttered muffin cups. Make a depression 1 inch wide and 1/2 inch deep in the center of each with a small spoon. Spoon 1 tablespoon chocolate hazelnut spread into each depression. Bake at 350 degrees for 20 minutes or until a wooden pick inserted into the muffin portion comes out with a few moist crumbs. Let cool in the muffin cups on a wire rack for 10 minutes. Loosen the muffins from the cups and move to a wire rack to cool completely.

Yield: 12 muffins

Dried Cherry Scones

These scones have a great flavor and a zip of cherry brandy.
Serve with Mock Devonshire Cream on page 135.

At Johnston Street Café, we made tons of scones from Bonnie Bailey's recipe. We added all kinds of flavors to the basic scone recipe. Bonnie was the owner of Highland Gourmet in Birmingham, Alabama, and continues to be a great friend, even helping me with one of our most popular cooking classes to date—The Thanksgiving Feast. She has two cookbooks of her own on the market, Remembrances of Things Passed, and her latest, Baking Secrets.

1/2 cup dried tart cherries
2 tablespoons cherry brandy
1 1/2 cups all-purpose flour
1/4 teaspoon salt
3 tablespoons plus
   2 teaspoons sugar
1 tablespoon baking powder
6 tablespoons butter, chilled
1 egg, beaten
1/3 cup plus 1 tablespoon
   half-and-half

Soak the cherries in the brandy for 15 minutes. Mix the flour, salt, 3 tablespoons of the sugar and the baking powder in a food processor. Add the butter and process until crumbly. Place in a large bowl. Combine the undrained cherries, egg and 1/3 cup of the half-and-half in a small bowl and mix gently. Add to the flour mixture and stir just until moistened. Place the dough on a lightly floured surface and knead twelve to fifteen times or until nearly smooth. Roll the dough lightly 3/4 inch thick. Cut into 2-inch circles, triangles or other desired shape. Place on an ungreased baking sheet. Brush the tops lightly with the remaining 1 tablespoon half-and-half. Sprinkle with the remaining 2 teaspoons sugar. Bake at 400 degrees for 12 to 15 minutes or until light brown.

Yield: 14 scones

Vanilla Cherry Scones

Serve with Mock Devonshire Cream (at right).
Cherry preserves would be nice, too.

2 cups all-purpose flour
^{1}/3 cup sugar
1 tablespoon baking powder
^{1}/2 teaspoon salt
6 tablespoons cold unsalted
    butter, cut into cubes
^{1}/3 cup heavy cream
2 egg yolks, lightly beaten
Seeds scraped from 1 large
    vanilla bean, or
    2 teaspoons vanilla extract
1 cup dried cherries,
    coarsely chopped
1 egg, lightly beaten
1 tablespoon milk
Sugar for sprinkling

Process the flour, ^{1}/3 cup sugar, the baking powder, salt and butter in a food processor until the mixture resembles coarse cornmeal. Combine the cream, egg yolks and vanilla bean seeds in a bowl and mix well. Stir in the dried cherries. Add to the flour mixture and knead briefly. Shape into a ball and place in the middle of a lined baking sheet. Pat or roll into a circle and cut into eight wedges. Brush with a mixture of the egg and milk. Sprinkle with sugar. Bake at 400 degrees for 20 minutes or until deep golden brown.

Yield: 8 large scones

To prepare Mock Devonshire Cream, stir ^{1}/4 cup sugar into 1 cup sour cream. Add 1 teaspoon vanilla extract and mix well. Spoon into a small crystal bowl.

Quick Cheese Bread

One of my very favorite quick breads is Quick Cheese Bread. Using Parmigiano-Reggiano cheese, which I always keep on hand, makes it so much better. Buy the chunks of Parmigiano-Reggiano cheese and grate in a food processor fitted with a steel blade. Be sure and cut off the wax covering from the wedge of cheese and cut into cubes before grating.

1 cup (4 ounces) Parmigiano-Reggiano cheese
3 cups unbleached all-purpose flour (15 ounces)
1 tablespoon baking powder
1/4 teaspoon cayenne pepper
1 teaspoon salt
1/8 teaspoon black pepper
4 ounces extra-sharp Cheddar cheese, cut into 1/2-inch cubes, or mild asiago cheese, crumbled into 1/2-inch pieces (about 1 cup)
1 1/4 cups milk
3 tablespoons unsalted butter, melted
1 egg, lightly beaten
3/4 cup sour cream

Spray a 5×9-inch loaf pan with nonstick cooking spray. Sprinkle 1/2 cup of the Parmigiano-Reggiano cheese evenly in the bottom of the pan. Whisk the flour, baking powder, cayenne pepper, salt and black pepper together in a large bowl. Add the Cheddar cheese and mix with a rubber spatula until the cheese is coated with flour, breaking up any clumps. Whisk the milk, butter, egg and sour cream together in a medium bowl. Fold gently into the cheese mixture with a rubber spatula just until mixed. The batter will be heavy and thick. Do not overmix. Scrape the batter into the prepared loaf pan, spreading to the sides of the pan and leveling the surface with a rubber spatula. Sprinkle the top evenly with the remaining 1/2 cup Parmigiano-Reggiano cheese. Bake on the middle oven rack at 350 degrees for 45 to 50 minutes or until deep golden brown and a wooden pick or skewer inserted into the center of the loaf comes out clean. Let cool in the pan on a wire rack for 5 minutes. Invert the loaf onto the wire rack to cool for 45 minutes or until warm. Cut into slices and serve.

Yield: 12 servings

Pull-Apart Cheesy Onion Bread

This is really fun to make and also yummy.

1/4 cup (1/2 stick) unsalted
   butter
1 large onion, finely
   chopped
1 tablespoon poppy seeds
Kosher salt and freshly
   ground pepper to taste
1 cup (4 ounces) coarsely
   shredded Gruyère
   cheese, asiago cheese
   or Swiss cheese
2 cups all-purpose flour
2 teaspoons baking powder
1/2 teaspoon baking soda
1 teaspoon salt
1/2 cup (1 stick) unsalted
   butter, cut into cubes
1 cup buttermilk

Melt 1/4 cup butter in a large skillet. Spoon
2 tablespoons of the melted butter into a small
bowl and reserve for brushing. Add the onion
to the remaining butter in the skillet. Cook
over medium heat for 8 minutes or until
softened, stirring occasionally. Stir in the
poppy seeds, kosher salt and pepper. Scrape
the onion mixture into a bowl. Chill for
5 minutes or until slightly cool. Stir in the
Gruyère cheese. Pulse the flour, baking powder,
baking soda and salt in a food processor. Add
the cubed butter and pulse until the mixture
resembles small peas. Add the buttermilk and
pulse five or six times, just until a soft dough
forms. Place the dough on a well-floured
surface and knead two or three times. Pat or
roll the dough into a 2×24-inch rectangle.
Spread the onion mixture on top. Cut the
dough crosswise into ten pieces. Stack nine
pieces onion-side up. Place the final piece
onion-side down on top of the stack. Lay the
stack carefully in a buttered 4×9-inch metal
loaf pan. Brush with the reserved butter. Bake
at 425 degrees on the center oven rack for
30 minutes or until risen and golden brown.
Let cool in the pan for 15 minutes. Invert
onto a serving plate and serve.

Yield: one 9-inch loaf

Cheddar and Stilton Drop Biscuits

Stilton cheese is the English contender for "King of Cheeses." Blue cheese can be substituted or even Gorgonzola. Homemade bread in a flash!

2 cups all-purpose flour
2 1/2 teaspoons baking powder
1 teaspoon salt
1/3 cup shortening, chilled
3/4 cup (3 ounces) mixed shredded Cheddar cheese and crumbled Stilton cheese
1 cup milk

Pulse the flour, baking powder and salt in a food processor to blend. Add the shortening and process until the dough is the consistency of cornmeal. Place in a bowl and add the cheese. Add the milk, stirring gently. Drop by spoonfuls onto a lined or greased baking sheet. Bake at 425 degrees for 12 to 15 minutes or until golden brown.

Yield: 20 medium biscuits

Spoon Bread

3 cups milk
1 1/2 cups sifted yellow cornmeal
1/2 cup (1 stick) butter, melted
Salt to taste
4 egg yolks
2 teaspoons baking powder
4 egg whites, stiffly beaten

Bring 2 cups of the milk to a boil in a saucepan. Whisk in the cornmeal gradually, adding in a steady stream. Stir in the butter and salt. Cook over low heat for 10 minutes, stirring almost constantly. Scrape into a mixing bowl and let cool to lukewarm. Beat the egg yolks in a bowl until light. Stir into the cornmeal mixture. Dissolve the baking powder in the remaining 1 cup milk and stir into the cornmeal mixture. Fold in the egg whites. Pour into a buttered 1 1/2-quart baking dish. Bake at 350 degrees for 40 minutes or until a knife inserted into the center comes out clean. Serve with butter.

Yield: 6 to 8 servings

Fresh Herb Spoon Rolls

1 envelope dry yeast
  (1 1/4 ounces)
2 cups warm water
  (110 degrees)
4 cups self-rising flour
3/4 cup (1 1/2 sticks) butter,
  melted
3/4 cup chopped fresh chives
1/4 cup dill weed
1/4 cup sugar
1 egg, lightly beaten

Dissolve the yeast in the warm water in a large bowl. Let stand for 5 minutes. Stir in the flour, butter, chives, dill weed, sugar and egg. Spoon into twenty-four lightly greased muffin cups, filling three-fourths full. Bake at 400 degrees for 20 to 25 minutes or until golden brown.

Yield: 2 dozen

Corn Pie with Roasted Red Peppers and Green Chiles

This is truly tasty and adds so much to a country dinner of veggies or is great with chili, stews, or soups.

2 (10-ounce) packages frozen
  corn kernels, thawed
1 cup (2 sticks) butter,
  melted
4 eggs, beaten
1 cup yellow cornmeal
2 teaspoons salt
1 cup sour cream
1 cup (4 ounces) shredded
  Swiss cheese
1 cup (4 ounces) shredded
  extra-sharp Cheddar
  cheese
1 (4-ounce) can chopped
  green chiles
1 (7-ounce) jar roasted red
  peppers, drained, rinsed
  and patted dry

Process the corn at low speed in a blender until partially puréed. Pour into a large mixing bowl. Add the butter, eggs, cornmeal, salt, sour cream, Swiss cheese, Cheddar cheese, green chiles and red peppers and mix well. Pour into a greased 10-inch deep-dish pie plate. Do not overfill. You may have a little extra batter that you can bake in custard cups. Bake at 375 degrees for 40 to 50 minutes or until firm to the touch and golden brown. Nonfat sour cream may be used in this recipe. If doubling the recipe, use three 9-inch pie plates.

Yield: 8 to 10 servings

Broccoli Corn Bread

Wow, this is easy and a great way to get children to eat their broccoli. I just love the flavor.

1 (8-ounce) package corn
  bread muffin mix
4 eggs
1 cup (4 ounces) shredded
  sharp Cheddar cheese
1/4 cup chopped onion
1 (10-ounce) package
  frozen broccoli florets,
  thawed and drained
1/2 cup (1 stick) butter,
  softened

Combine the muffin mix, eggs, cheese, onion, broccoli and butter in a large bowl and mix well. Pour into a greased 10-inch cast-iron skillet. Bake at 375 degrees for 35 minutes or until golden brown.

Yield: 10 to 12 servings

Roast Beef Tenderloin

*Greg Clemons, CPA, a wonderful person and one of my
dedicated assistants, cooks a "mean" beef tenderloin. He can clean and
strip the "silver" on a tenderloin in a flash.*

1 (6- to 8-pound) beef
   tenderloin
Salt and cracked pepper
   to taste
1 cup olive oil
1/2 cup red wine
1 teaspoon minced garlic
5 tablespoons cracked pepper

Sprinkle the beef with salt and pepper to taste and place in a shallow dish or bowl. Whisk the olive oil, wine, garlic and 3 tablespoons of the pepper in a bowl. Pour over the beef. Marinate in the refrigerator for 1 hour. Drain the beef, discarding the marinade. Place the beef on a rack in a roasting pan. Rub with the remaining 2 tablespoons pepper. Roast at 500 degrees for 5 minutes. Reduce the oven temperature to 400 degrees. Roast for 40 to 45 minutes or to the desired degree of doness.

Yield: 10 to 12 servings

*Stripping the silver means
using a very sharp
knife to cut off the tough
silvery covering plus
extra fat on the tenderloin.
For a rare tenderloin, roast
the beef until it reaches
135 to 140 degrees on a
meat thermometer. Roast
to 155 to 160 degrees for
medium or to 165 to
170 degrees for well done.
Let stand for 10 minutes
before serving.*

Asian Flank Steak

*A flank steak has a wonderful flavor and is very tender if it is
not overcooked and is cut on the bias.*

1/4 cup sherry
1/4 cup low-sodium soy sauce
1/4 cup honey
2 tablespoons white vinegar
1 tablespoon minced
   fresh ginger
1 tablespoon dark sesame oil
2 garlic cloves, crushed
1 pound lean flank steak

Combine the sherry, soy sauce, honey, vinegar, ginger, sesame oil and garlic in a sealable plastic bag. Add the steak and seal the bag, turning to coat. Marinate in the refrigerator for 8 hours. Drain the steak, reserving the marinade. Place the steak on a grill or broiler rack coated with nonstick cooking spray. Grill or broil for 8 minutes on each side or to the desired degree of doneness. Do not overcook. Pour the reserved marinade in a saucepan. Bring to a boil over medium heat and boil for 3 minutes. Cut the steak diagonally into slices and serve with the cooked marinade.

Yield: 6 to 8 servings

Beef Medallions with Cognac Sauce

This recipe provides an exceptionally delicious meal for a very special occasion. When you are scraping up the brown bits on the bottom of the pan, you are deglazing the pan.

6 tablespoons unsalted butter
3/4 cup chopped shallots
1 tablespoon brown sugar
3 cups canned low-sodium
   chicken broth
1 1/2 cups canned beef broth
3/4 cup Cognac or brandy
3/4 cup whipping cream
6 (4- to 5-ounce) filets
   mignons or tenderloin
   steaks (each about
   1 inch thick)
Salt and pepper to taste
Fresh chives for garnish

Melt 3 tablespoons of the butter in a heavy medium saucepan over medium heat. Add the shallots and sauté for 4 minutes or until tender. Add the brown sugar and cook for 1 minute, stirring constantly. Add the chicken broth, beef broth and Cognac. Simmer for 20 minutes or until the sauce is reduced to 1/2 cup. Stir in the cream. Sprinkle the beef with salt and pepper. Melt the remaining 3 tablespoons butter in a heavy medium skillet over medium-high heat. Add the steaks. Cook for 4 minutes on each side for rare or to the desired degree of doneness. Remove the steaks to plates. Pour the sauce into the drippings in the skillet. Bring to a boil, scraping up any browned bits. Sprinkle with salt and pepper. Cut the steaks into slices and fan the slices on serving plates. Top with the sauce and garnish with chives.

Yield: 6 servings

Deglazing the Pan

After sautéing or roasting, look at the bottom of the pan. Those dark food particles stuck to the bottom are caramelized drippings from meat juices. This is called "fond," a French term loosely meaning bottom or foundation. Loaded with flavor, it can be used to make gravy. Add any liquid and start scraping vigorously.

Alan's Cajun Meat Loaf

*Alan and Frankie Freeze served this delicious meat loaf when
they had us to dinner in Ketchum.*

2 green onions, finely
  chopped
1 cup finely chopped onion
1/2 cup finely chopped green
  bell pepper
1/3 cup finely chopped celery
1 tablespoon minced garlic
2 tablespoons butter
1 1/2 teaspoons salt
1 teaspoon ground cumin
1/2 teaspoon freshly ground
  black pepper
1/2 teaspoon cayenne pepper
1/8 teaspoon nutmeg
2 bay leaves
1/2 cup ketchup
1/2 cup half-and-half
1 pound ground beef
1 pound ground pork
2 eggs, lightly beaten
2 teaspoons Worcestershire
  sauce
1 1/2 teaspoons Tabasco sauce

Sauté the green onions, onion, bell pepper,
celery and garlic in the butter in a skillet until
softened. Add the salt, cumin, black pepper,
cayenne pepper, nutmeg and bay leaves and
cook for 1 minute. Add the ketchup and half-
and-half and cook for 2 minutes. Discard the
bay leaves. Combine the ground beef, pork,
eggs, Worcestershire sauce and Tabasco sauce
in a large bowl and mix well. Add the vegetable
mixture and mix well. Spoon evenly in a
5×9-inch loaf pan. Bake at 350 degrees for
70 minutes or to 160 degrees on a meat
thermometer. Let stand until cool. Drain
before serving.

Yield: 6 servings

Pork Tenderloin Wrapped in Bacon with Blackberry Chutney Sauce

Wild blackberries that I picked at our farm as a child had delicious, small-seeded berries. The berries with huge seeds we use now are called dew berries. This sauce is good made using either berry.

1 cup apple juice
1 tablespoon balsamic
   vinegar
1 bay leaf
2 tablespoons brown sugar
1/8 teaspoon cinnamon
1 teaspoon kosher salt
1/4 teaspoon freshly
   ground pepper
2 whole pork tenderloins,
   cleaned and trimmed
8 to 10 slices thin-cut bacon
Blackberry Chutney Sauce
   (at right)

Combine the apple juice, vinegar, bay leaf, brown sugar, cinnamon, salt and pepper in a saucepan and mix well. Heat just until the brown sugar melts. Remove from the heat to cool. Place the pork in a sealable plastic bag. Pour the cooled marinade over the pork and seal the bag. Marinate in the refrigerator for 2 to 3 hours, turning several times to ensure that all surfaces are covered. Drain the pork, discarding the marinade and pat dry. Wrap the bacon firmly around the pork in a spiral direction, beginning at one end and making sure to cover the entire surface. Place the pork on a grill rack. Grill over medium direct heat (300 to 350 degrees) for 8 minutes or until seared, turning one-quarter turn every 2 to 3 minutes. Grill over medium indirect heat for 15 to 20 minutes longer or until the pork is cooked through. Remove from the grill and let rest for 5 minutes. Cut on a slight angle into slices 1 inch thick. Serve with Blackberry Chutney Sauce.

Yield: 6 to 8 servings

Blackberry Chutney Sauce

1 cup minced shallot
1 cup chopped onion
1 tablespoon
   unsalted butter
2 cups fresh or
   frozen blackberries
1/4 cup sugar
1/2 cup blackberry preserves
2 tablespoons apple
   cider vinegar
1 tablespoon
   cracked pepper
1 tablespoon minced garlic
1 cinnamon stick

Cook the shallot and onion in the butter in a 1 1/2-quart heavy saucepan over moderate heat for 3 to 5 minutes or until golden brown, stirring occasionally. Stir in the remaining ingredients. Simmer for 20 minutes or until the berries burst and the sauce is thickened. Strain through a fine mesh sieve or metal strainer into a bowl, discarding the solids. Let cool to room temperature.

Yield: about 4 cups

Pulled Pork

An easy, super recipe for pulled pork sandwiches, and you can be gone all day while this tasty pork cooks. Be sure your sauce is not thick. If it is, dilute the 1¹/2 cups sauce a bit with water and serve the thicker sauce on the side. You may add herbs to the barbecue sauce.

1 (2¹/2- to 4-pound)
   pork loin, trimmed
1¹/2 cups barbecue
   sauce, plus additional
   for serving

Cut the pork into halves and place side by side in a slow cooker. Pour the sauce over the pork. Cook, covered, on Low for 8 to 10 hours or until 160 degrees on a meat thermometer. Pull the pork into shreds using two forks. Serve as a main entrée or on buns for a barbecue fare. Serve with additional sauce.

Yield: 8 servings

Fruit-Stuffed Pork Loin

This is delicious, but I will have to say, when we were preparing it in class everyone got tickled as I pushed the prunes into the loin with a wooden spoon. Pork loin is usually an inexpensive cut of meat.

¹/2 cup dried prunes
   and apricots
1 (4-pound) boneless center-
   cut pork loin roast
¹/2 teaspoon salt
Coarsely ground pepper
   to taste
¹/3 cup olive oil
2 carrots, chopped
1 large yellow onion,
   chopped
2 ribs celery, chopped
1 head garlic, cut into halves
6 slices bacon, finely
   chopped
1 sprig of rosemary
3 sprigs of sage
¹/2 cup white wine
1 cup chicken stock
2 tablespoons unsalted
   butter

Press the dried fruit into the center length of the pork loin using the handle of a wooden spoon. Work from both ends until the dried fruit has been threaded throughout. Sprinkle with the salt and pepper. Heat a roasting pan over high heat for 2 minutes. Heat the olive oil in the roasting pan until it begins to smoke. Add the pork and brown evenly on each side for 3 to 4 minutes or until deep brown. Add the carrots, onion, celery, garlic, bacon, rosemary and sage. Roast at 450 degrees for 40 minutes or to 160 degrees on a meat thermometer for a moist roast with a touch of rosy color. Let rest for 15 minutes before slicing. Heat the drippings in the roasting pan over medium heat. Add the wine. Bring to a boil, stirring with a wooden spoon to scrape the brown bits from the bottom of the pan. Add the stock. Cook until the liquid is reduced by one-third. Swirl in the butter. Strain the sauce, discarding the solids. Keep the au jus warm while carving the pork. Serve the pork with the au jus passed alongside.

Yield: 10 servings

Garlic White Lasagna

1¹/2 pounds hot Italian
    sausage, casings removed
4 large garlic cloves, chopped
1 onion, chopped
1 (12-ounce) jar roasted
    red peppers, drained
    and chopped
¹/2 cup white wine,
    such as chardonnay
1 (10-ounce) package frozen
    chopped spinach
15 ounces ricotta cheese
¹/2 teaspoon salt
¹/2 teaspoon pepper
1 egg, lightly beaten
2 (17-ounce) jars creamy
    Alfredo sauce
12 uncooked lasagna noodles
12 ounces mozzarella
    cheese, sliced
1 cup (4 ounces) finely
    grated Parmesan cheese

Brown the sausage in a large skillet over
medium heat, stirring with a wooden spoon
until crumbly. Remove the sausage and set
aside. Reserve 1 tablespoon of the drippings in
the skillet. Cook the garlic and onion in the
reserved drippings over medium-high heat until
the onion is tender. Stir in the sausage, red
peppers and wine. Bring to a boil. Reduce the
heat and simmer, uncovered, for 5 minutes or
until most of the liquid has evaporated. Cook
the spinach using the package directions.
Drain and squeeze between paper towels to
remove the excess liquid. Combine the spinach,
ricotta cheese, salt, pepper and egg in a bowl
and mix well. Spread 1 cup of the Alfredo
sauce in a greased 9×13-inch baking dish.
Layer four uncooked noodles, one-half of the
spinach mixture and one-half of the sausage
mixture in the prepared dish. Layer four slices
of the mozzarella cheese over the sausage.
Continue layering with 1 cup of the remaining
Alfredo sauce, one-half of the remaining
noodles, the remaining spinach mixture and
remaining sausage mixture. Top with the
remaining noodles and mozzarella cheese
slices. Spread the remaining Alfredo sauce over
the top and sprinkle with the Parmesan cheese.
Chill, covered, for 8 to 10 hours, if desired.
Let stand at room temperature for 30 minutes
before baking. Bake, covered, at 350 degrees
for 45 minutes. Bake, uncovered, for
15 minutes longer. Let stand for 15 minutes
before serving.

Yield: 8 servings

Venison Medallions in a Veal Stock

The one and only, Rick Paler, great chef, especially with wild game and gourmet recipes, presents these medallions. We have a ball with the Wild Game Class featuring Rick, Judge Sherrie Paler, and Joe Propst.

1 loin or tenderloin of
    venison, cut into
    1/2-inch medallions
Buttermilk
Kosher salt and freshly
    cracked pepper for
    sprinkling
1/4 cup (1/2 stick) butter
1/4 cup vegetable oil
1/4 cup chopped shallots
2 tablespoons red wine
2 tablespoons Calvados
    or Cognac
1 cup veal stock
1 cup fresh apple cider
6 tablespoons butter,
    softened

Soak the venison in buttermilk in a bowl in the refrigerator for 8 to 10 hours. Drain and pat dry with a paper towel. Liberally sprinkle both sides with salt and pepper and press into the venison. Melt 1/4 cup butter with the oil in a skillet over high heat and heat until bubbly. Add the medallions and sear for 2 to 3 minutes on each side or until medium-rare. Remove to a warm platter and keep warm. Add the shallots to the drippings in the skillet and shake for 20 seconds. Add the wine and scrape the brown bits from the bottom of the skillet. Add the Calvados. Ignite and let the flames subside. Add the stock. Bring to a boil. Boil until the mixture is reduced by one-half. Add the cider and return to a boil. Boil until the mixture is reduced by one-half. Remove the skillet from the heat. Add 6 tablespoons butter 2 tablespoons at a time shaking the skillet from side to side until melted and well mixed. Do not stir. Place the medallions on a serving plate and spoon the sauce over the top. Serve with Braised Apples on page 128. Pork tenderloin medallions may be used instead of the venison medallions.

Yield: 8 servings

Chicken Divan

My friend, Noel Shin, who is talented both in the kitchen and in the art studio, makes this Chicken Divan with the delectable Béchamel Sauce instead of using chicken soup. What a dish for family or for entertaining! Béchamel Sauce is a basic French white sauce. It is the basis for countless dishes. The egg yolks are added for richness.

2 (10-ounce) packages
    frozen broccoli
6 bone-in chicken breasts,
    cooked and deboned
Béchamel Sauce (below)
1/2 cup grated Parmigiano-
    Reggiano cheese

Cook the broccoli using the package directions; drain. Arrange the broccoli in a 3-quart baking dish. Debone the chicken. Place over the broccoli. Pour the Béchamel Sauce over the chicken. Sprinkle with the cheese. Bake at 350 degrees for 15 minutes.

Béchamel Sauce

1/4 cup (1/2 stick)
    unsalted butter
1/4 cup all-purpose flour
2 cups milk
2 egg yolks, beaten
1/3 cup dry sherry wine
11/2 teaspoons salt
1/2 teaspoon freshly
    ground pepper

Melt the butter in a saucepan over medium heat. Do not brown. Add the flour and whisk until blended. Whisk in the milk. Cook over medium heat until thickened, whisking constantly. Add the egg yolks, wine, salt and pepper and whisk until blended and egg yolks are cooked.

Panéed Chicken with Pecan Meunière Sauce

One of my favorite people, Vicki McCain, owner of Kitchenique in Destin, Florida, where I do many cooking classes each year, contributed this delicious recipe. Teaching at Vicki's has been a great experience and a good excuse to go to Destin.

4 boneless skinless chicken breasts
Sea salt and white pepper to taste
Wondra flour for coating
2 tablespoons grapeseed oil, peanut oil or olive oil
Pecan Meunière Sauce (below)

Sprinkle the chicken lightly with sea salt and white pepper. Dredge in the flour and shake off the excess. Heat the oil in a large nonstick sauté pan over medium-high heat. Add the chicken when a pinch of flour sizzles or the oil begins to smoke. Cook on one side for 3 minutes or until brown. Turn and cook the remaining side until brown and cooked through. Place on an oven rack. Keep warm in a 250-degree oven until serving time. Serve with Pecan Meunière Sauce.

Yield: 4 servings

Pecan Meunière Sauce

4 ounces whole pecans
1/2 cup (1 stick) unsalted butter
1 teaspoon pressed garlic
Juice of 1/2 lemon (about 2 tablespoons)
2 tablespoons parsley

Spread the pecans in a single layer on a baking sheet. Roast at 350 degrees for 10 to 15 minutes or until brown. Remove from the oven to cool. Coarsely chop the pecans. Melt the butter over medium heat in a saucepan. Cook until the butter begins to brown, stirring constantly. Remove from the heat. Add the garlic and lemon juice. Return to the heat. Add the pecans and stir constantly until the foam subsides. Stir in the parsley and serve.

Grilled Chicken
à la Suzie and Steve

*This chicken is so moist and tender. Be sure to buy plump
breasts of chicken—good quality and on the bone. Steve and Suzie Powers
are from Philadelphia, Pennsylvania, and Ketchum, Idaho. They are
wonderful hosts and always entertain us royally.*

8 bone-in chicken breasts
Salt to taste
1 tablespoon coriander seeds
1 tablespoon yellow
    mustard seeds
2 teaspoons fennel seeds
1/4 cup Hungarian
    sweet paprika
3 teaspoons salt
3 teaspoons pepper
Sauce (below)

Season the chicken lightly with salt. Pulse
the coriander, mustard and fennel seeds in a
food processor until finely ground. Add the
paprika, 3 teaspoons salt and the pepper and
pulse to combine. Rub the seasoning mixture
over the chicken. Chill, covered, for 8 hours.
Arrange the chicken on a preheated 450-degree
grill. Grill with the cover closed for 2 minutes
on each side. Reduce the temperature to
350 degrees and grill for 30 to 45 minutes,
or until cooked through, turning occasionally.
Serve with the Sauce.

Yield: 8 servings

Sauce

1/2 cup sherry wine vinegar
3 tablespoons Dijon mustard
1 1/3 cups olive oil
3/4 cup chopped chives
1/4 cup chopped fresh
    tarragon
Salt and pepper to taste

Combine the vinegar and Dijon mustard in a
bowl and whisk until blended. Add the olive oil
gradually, whisking constantly. Add the chives,
tarragon, salt and pepper and mix well.

149 | *Entrées*

Party Chicken, Shrimp and Artichoke Casserole

Elegant and delicious, this is a great casserole to make for a crowd. It can be assembled the day before your party and chilled for 8 to 10 hours. Remove from the refrigerator an hour before baking. A bread, green salad, and dessert finish the menu.

3 pounds fresh domestic white mushrooms
Butter for sautéing
8 whole chicken breasts, cooked and cut into large pieces
2 pounds peeled cooked shrimp, or 4 pounds shrimp in the shell, boiled and peeled
3 (14-ounce) cans artichoke hearts, cut into quarters
Medium White Sauce (below)
2 tablespoons Worcestershire sauce
1 cup sherry or white wine
1 cup (4 ounces) freshly grated Parmigiano-Reggiano cheese

Sauté the mushrooms in butter in a skillet until tender. Divide the chicken, shrimp, artichokes and mushrooms equally among two greased 3-quart or 9×13-inch baking dishes. Mix the Medium White Sauce, Worcestershire sauce and sherry in a bowl. Pour over the layers in the baking dishes. Top each with 1/2 cup of the cheese. Bake, uncovered, at 375 degrees for 30 minutes or until bubbly.

Yield: 18 to 20 servings

Medium White Sauce

1 cup (2 sticks) unsalted butter
1 cup all-purpose flour
6 cups milk
1 tablespoon salt
1 teaspoon white pepper

Melt the butter in a heavy medium saucepan over medium heat. Add the flour and continue to heat until bubbly, stirring constantly. Whisk in the milk gradually. Cook until thickened, stirring constantly. Add the salt and white pepper.

Yield: 6 cups

Shrimp Fettuccini

Wow, when I'm feeling really thin and hungry for something creamy, this is delicious and satisfying. Leave out the shrimp and add crumbled bacon for Fettuccini Carbonara.

5 green onions, chopped
2 cups sliced mushrooms
2 garlic cloves, minced
1/2 cup (1 stick) butter
2 tablespoons vegetable oil
1 pound peeled shrimp
2 teaspoons salt
8 ounces fettuccini
Salt to taste
3/4 cup (3 ounces) grated
   Romano cheese
3/4 cup (3 ounces) grated
   Parmigiano-Reggiano
   cheese
1 cup heavy cream
1/4 cup chopped parsley

Sauté the green onions, mushrooms and garlic in 1/4 cup of the butter and the oil in a large skillet over medium heat until the mushrooms are tender. Add the shrimp. Sauté until the shrimp turn pink, pouring off some of the liquid if needed. Sprinkle with 2 teaspoons salt. Cover and keep warm. Do not overcook the shrimp. Cook the pasta in boiling salted water in a saucepan until tender. Melt the remaining 1/4 cup butter in a saucepan. Drain the pasta and toss with the melted butter. Add the Romano cheese, Parmigiano-Reggiano cheese and cream and mix well. Add to the shrimp mixture and toss to mix. Sprinkle with the parsley and serve immediately.

Yield: 4 to 6 servings

Maple-Glazed Salmon with Pineapple Salsa

Full of omega-3 oil, this recipe will help keep your cholesterol in check. I adore salmon and prefer wild salmon over pond-raised salmon for health reasons.

6 (6-ounce) salmon fillets
6 tablespoons maple syrup
6 tablespoons teriyaki sauce
6 tablespoons pineapple juice
2 tablespoons minced
   fresh ginger
6 garlic cloves, crushed
6 tablespoons bourbon
Pineapple Salsa (below)

Place the salmon in a sealable plastic bag. Mix the maple syrup, teriyaki sauce, pineapple juice, ginger, garlic and bourbon in a bowl. Pour over the salmon and seal the bag. Marinate in the refrigerator for 1 to 10 hours. Drain the salmon, discarding the marinade. Place the salmon in a grill basket sprayed with nonstick cooking spray. Grill skin side down over hot coals for 15 to 20 minutes or until the salmon flakes easily. Do not turn. Serve with Pineapple Salsa.

Yield: 6 servings

Pineapple Salsa

5 tomatoes, chopped
3/4 cup chopped bell pepper
2 jalapeño chiles,
   finely chopped
1 1/2 cups pineapple chunks
1 teaspoon salt
2 teaspoons sugar
3 tablespoons white vinegar

Combine the tomatoes, bell pepper, jalapeño chiles, pineapple, salt, sugar and vinegar in a small saucepan. Simmer over low heat for 5 minutes. Remove from the heat to cool. Chill, covered with plastic wrap, until serving time.

Yield: 6 servings

Mushroom Lasagna with Gorgonzola Sauce

One of my very favorite dishes to accompany any beef recipe.
Every time I serve it, people ask for the recipe.

3/4 cup (1 1/2 sticks) butter
2 tablespoons olive oil
2 shallots, minced
2 garlic cloves, minced
1 pound white domestic
   mushrooms, sliced
8 ounces fresh shiitake
   mushrooms, portabello
   mushrooms or a mixture
   of each, stems removed
   and caps sliced
   1/4 inch thick
1 1/2 teaspoons salt
1/2 teaspoon freshly ground
   black pepper
1/2 teaspoon dried tarragon
Cayenne pepper to taste
2 tablespoons fresh lemon
   juice
1/2 cup (1 stick) butter
1/2 cup all-purpose flour
2 cups milk
1 cup heavy cream
3 ounces Gorgonzola cheese,
   crumbled
1 cup (4 ounces) freshly
   grated Parmesan cheese
1 teaspoon salt
16 ounces no-boil lasagna
   noodles
1 tablespoon butter

Melt 3/4 cup butter in a large skillet. Add the olive oil. Add the shallots, garlic and mushrooms. Cook for 5 to 7 minutes or until the liquid evaporates, stirring frequently. Add 1 1/2 teaspoons salt, the black pepper, tarragon, cayenne pepper and lemon juice; mix well. Melt 1/2 cup butter in a saucepan over medium heat. Add the flour. Cook for 2 to 3 minutes without letting the flour turn color, stirring constantly. Whisk in the milk and cream. Bring to a boil. Cook until thickened and smooth, whisking constantly. Reduce the heat and simmer for 5 minutes, whisking frequently. Add the Gorgonzola cheese and 1/2 cup of the Parmesan cheese. Cook until melted, stirring constantly. Add 1 teaspoon salt and cayenne pepper. Keep warm over low heat. Spread a layer of the sauce in a 9×13-inch baking pan buttered or sprayed with nonstick cooking spray. Layer one-third of the noodles and one-half of the mushroom mixture over the sauce. Drizzle 1 cup of the remaining sauce over the mushrooms. Continue with a layer of half the remaining noodles, the remaining mushroom mixture and one-half of the remaining sauce. Top with the remaining noodles. Pour the remaining sauce over the layers. Sprinkle with the remaining 1/2 cup Parmesan cheese. Dot with 1 tablespoon butter. Bake at 375 degrees for 30 minutes or until bubbly and light brown on top. The lasagna may chilled, covered, for 8 to 10 hours or frozen for up to two weeks. Bring to room temperature before baking.

Yield: 10 to 12 servings

Asparagus

Asparagus is my favorite vegetable. If you do not have an asparagus bed, you might give it a try as it is certainly a fun garden item. Plant in well-drained, sandy soil. It takes three years to produce properly. It produces shoots in the early spring until hot weather. Asparagus must be cut back in the fall just before frost and covered with manure or mulch.

Stir-Fry Sauce

My children absolutely love this, so I always keep a jar of marinade in the refrigerator or freezer. Try it with chicken, pork, or beef.

3 tablespoons dark
  brown sugar
1/3 cup cornstarch
2 teaspoons minced fresh
  ginger, or 2 teaspoons
  ground ginger
4 garlic cloves, crushed
1/2 cup naturally brewed
  soy sauce
1/2 cup sherry
1/4 teaspoon bottled red
  pepper sauce
3 tablespoons red wine
2 1/2 cups beef broth or
  chicken broth

Mix the brown sugar, cornstarch, ginger, garlic, soy sauce, sherry, red pepper sauce, wine and broth in a 1-quart jar. Store in the refrigerator for three weeks, or freeze in 1-cup portions for later use. To use, sauté 1 pound chicken strips, beef strips or pork strips in 1 tablespoon olive oil in a wok until brown. Remove from the wok and set aside. Sauté 4 cups of vegetables of choice (such as chopped onions, chopped squash or chopped broccoli) in the wok until tender. Return the meat to the wok and add 1 cup or more of the stir-fry sauce. Simmer until the sauce thickens and the meat is done. Serve over hot cooked rice.

Yield: about 3 cups

Roasted Asparagus with Almonds and Asiago Cheese

1 1/2 pounds pencil-thin
  asparagus spears
3 tablespoons extra-virgin
  olive oil
Salt and freshly ground
  pepper to taste
1/3 cup sliced almonds
2 ounces asiago cheese or
  Parmesan cheese, shaved
  (1/2 cup)

Toss the asparagus with the olive oil on a large rimmed baking sheet. Sprinkle with salt and pepper. Roast at 400 degrees for 15 minutes or until tender. Spread the almonds in a round shallow baking dish. Bake for 5 minutes or until toasted and golden brown. Place the asparagus on a platter. Sprinkle with salt and pepper. Scatter the cheese over the asparagus. Sprinkle with the almonds. If you prefer to serve thicker asparagus spears, add about 10 minutes to the roasting time.

Yield: 8 servings

Green Beans with Caramelized Shallots

"Haricots verts" is French for small green beans. Shallots are a combo of onion and garlic but more subtly flavored—more mild.

2 pounds haricots verts or
   slender green beans,
   trimmed
Salt to taste
8 ounces shallots
2 tablespoons butter
2 tablespoons olive oil
1/4 teaspoon dried thyme
Ground pepper to taste

Cook the haricots verts in boiling salted water in a saucepan for 4 minutes or until tender and drain. Plunge immediately into ice water to cool. Drain well. Cut off and discard the ends from the shallots. Cut the shallots lengthwise into halves. Melt the butter and olive oil in a large heavy skillet over medium-high heat. Add the shallots and sauté for 1 minute. Reduce the heat to medium-low. Sauté for 20 minutes longer or until brown and tender. Sprinkle with the thyme, salt and pepper. Add the haricots verts and cook until heated through. The haricots verts may be made one day ahead. Wrap in several layers of paper towels and place in a sealable plastic bag. Seal the bag and chill until ready to use.

Yield: 6 to 8 servings

Creamy Red Beans and Rice with Caramelized Onions

Easy, easy—a quick, stir-together side dish.

2 tablespoons butter
1 large onion, sliced
3 cups hot cooked rice
1 (16-ounce) can red kidney
   beans, drained
2¹/2 cups sour cream
3¹/2 cups (14 ounces) grated
   asiago cheese
4¹/2 teaspoons freshly
   ground pepper

Melt the butter in a skillet over medium heat. Add the onion. Cook for 8 minutes or until the onion begins to brown. Add the rice, beans, sour cream, cheese and pepper. Cook until the cheese is melted, stirring constantly.

Yield: 8 servings

Broccoli-Parmesan Gratin

We don't care if President George H. W. Bush didn't like broccoli.
We do! This recipe is easy and tasty.

1 bunch broccoli
   (about 1¹/2 pounds)
1 quart water
1 teaspoon salt
1 cup milk
¹/2 cup heavy cream
1 cup (4 ounces) grated
   Parmigiano-Reggiano
   cheese
2 eggs
¹/2 teaspoon salt
¹/2 teaspoon ground pepper
1 cup coarse bread crumbs
1 tablespoon extra-virgin
   olive oil
Pinch of salt
Pinch of ground pepper

Cut the broccoli into 1-inch pieces. Peel the large stems with a knife and cut into rounds ¹/2 inch thick. Bring 1 quart water with 1 teaspoon salt to a boil in a saucepan. Add the broccoli. Cook for 5 minutes and drain. Place the broccoli in a 2-quart shallow flameproof baking dish. Whisk the milk, cream, cheese, eggs, ¹/2 teaspoon salt and ¹/2 teaspoon pepper together in a bowl. Pour over the broccoli. Toss the bread crumbs with the olive oil. Add a pinch of salt and pinch of pepper. Sprinkle evenly over the gratin. Bake at 350 degrees for 30 minutes or until set. Broil for 2 to 3 minutes or until the bread crumbs are golden brown. Let stand for 5 minutes before serving. Use 1 teaspoon salt for every 1 quart of water when cooking the broccoli. You may also use an equivalent amount of frozen broccoli, thawed.

Yield: 6 servings

Brussels Sprouts with Prosciutto and Parmesan Cheese

Although I am not really fond of brussels sprouts, this is very good.
Bacon can be used instead of prosciutto.

3 tablespoons butter
2 garlic cloves, minced
3 ounces thinly sliced
  prosciutto or bacon, cut
  into slivers
1¹/2 pounds brussels sprouts,
  trimmed and halved
2 tablespoons all-purpose
  flour
1¹/2 cups light cream (half-
  and-half)
3 tablespoons marsala
³/4 teaspoon grated nutmeg
Salt and freshly ground
  pepper to taste
³/4 cup (3 ounces) grated
  Parmesan cheese

Melt the butter in a large skillet over medium-high heat. Add the garlic and prosciutto and sauté for 2 minutes. Add the brussels sprouts and cook for 5 minutes. Add the flour, stirring to coat the brussels sprouts. Stir in the cream and wine gradually. Reduce the heat to a simmer. Simmer, covered, for 12 to 15 minutes or until the brussels sprouts are tender. Sprinkle with the nutmeg, salt and pepper. Stir in ¹/2 cup of the cheese. Cook just until the cheese is melted. Remove from the heat. Spoon into an oval baking dish. Top with the remaining ¹/4 cup cheese. Bake at 350 degrees for 20 minutes or until bubbly and the top is slightly brown. Serve hot.

Yield: 6 to 8 servings

Tasty Collard Greens

How healthy those collard greens are! This recipe, for those who do not like collard greens, actually is flavored so well that you will enjoy them—and think of the vitamins you're getting, especially your dose of iron.

6 slices bacon, chopped
1 sweet onion, chopped
1 tablespoon canola oil
1 (16-ounce) package fresh
  collard greens, trimmed
1 (12-ounce) can light beer
2 tablespoons balsamic
  vinegar
1 tablespoon butter
1 teaspoon salt
¹/2 teaspoon pepper

Fry the bacon and onion in the canola oil in a large heavy saucepan over medium-high heat for 5 minutes or until the onion is tender. Add the collards in batches and cook for 5 minutes or until wilted. Stir in the beer. Bring to a boil. Reduce the heat to low. Cook for 25 minutes or to the desired degree of tenderness, stirring occasionally. Stir in the vinegar, butter, salt and pepper.

Yield: 6 to 8 servings

Creamy Mashed Potatoes with Caramelized Onions

Caramelized onions give these mashed potatoes a real "doozy" of a topping. Tasty and attractive.

2¹/2 pounds Yukon Gold
   baking potatoes
Salt to taste
2 tablespoons extra-virgin
   olive oil
2 large onions, thinly sliced
   or chopped
3 tablespoons balsamic
   vinegar
2 tablespoons brown sugar
Black pepper to taste
¹/2 cup (1 stick) unsalted
   butter, softened and cut up
¹/2 cup whipping cream,
   half-and-half or milk,
   warmed
Freshly grated nutmeg
   to taste
White pepper to taste
1 tablespoon chopped
   fresh parsley

Peel and quarter the potatoes. Place the potatoes in boiling salted water to cover in a large saucepan. Cook, covered, for 20 minutes or until tender; drain. Heat the olive oil in a large skillet. Add the onions. Cook over medium-low heat until very tender, stirring occasionally. Add the vinegar and brown sugar. Cook for 5 minutes. Remove from the heat. Sprinkle with salt and black pepper. Mash the potatoes in a bowl. Return to the saucepan. Stir in the butter and whipping cream. Sprinkle with nutmeg, salt and white pepper. Spoon the potatoes into a serving bowl. Top with the caramelized onions. Sprinkle with the parsley.

Yield: 6 to 8 servings

Spinach Casserole

Easily stirred up with lots of vitamins. Popeye would love it and so will you.

2 (10-ounce) packages
    frozen chopped
    spinach, thawed
6 tablespoons butter, melted
2 cups milk
1 cup saltine cracker crumbs
1 onion, chopped
3 eggs, beaten
Salt to taste
1 cup (4 ounces) shredded
    sharp Cheddar cheese

Drain the spinach and squeeze out all of the excess moisture. Pour the butter over the spinach in a bowl and mix well. Combine the milk, cracker crumbs and onion in a bowl and mix well. Add to the spinach mixture and mix well. Stir in the eggs and salt. Spoon into a buttered 2-quart baking dish. Place the dish in a larger pan and fill the outer pan with enough boiling water to come halfway up the sides of the baking dish. Bake at 350 degrees for 40 minutes. Sprinkle the cheese over the top. Bake for 5 minutes.

Yield: 8 to 10 servings

Great Stuffed Sweet Potatoes

You could use pineapple tidbits instead of the raisins if you prefer.

6 sweet potatoes
    (3 1/2 pounds)
1/2 cup coarsely chopped
    pecans
1/2 cup (1 stick) butter
1 large Rome Beauty
    apple, chopped
1/2 cup golden raisins
1 cup firmly packed
    brown sugar
1 teaspoon cinnamon
1/2 teaspoon nutmeg

Place the sweet potatoes on a foil-lined baking sheet. Bake at 425 degrees for 1 1/4 hours or until tender. Heat the pecans in a nonstick skillet over medium-low heat for 5 minutes or until toasted, stirring frequently. Remove from the skillet. Melt the butter in a skillet over medium-high heat. Add the apple and raisins. Sauté for 2 to 3 minutes or until the apple is tender. Stir in the brown sugar, cinnamon and nutmeg. Remove from the heat. Cut the sweet potatoes into halves lengthwise. Scoop the pulp into a large bowl, leaving the shells intact. Add the apple mixture and stir to combine. Spoon into the reserved shells. Place on a baking sheet. Bake at 325 degrees for 15 minutes or until heated through. Sprinkle with the pecans.

Yield: 8 servings

Oven-Roasted Seasonal Vegetables

You use less of dried herbs than of fresh, so when converting
to fresh, add twice the amount of dried. If the recipe calls for 2 teaspoons
of dried thyme, add 4 teaspoons of fresh.

1 cup olive oil
6 garlic cloves, chopped
2 tablespoons fresh rosemary
   leaves, chopped
2 tablespoons fresh thyme
   leaves, chopped
1/2 teaspoon salt
1/2 teaspoon pepper
2 sweet potatoes, peeled and
   cut into thick slices
2 yellow squash,
   cut into thick slices
2 zucchini, cut into
   thick slices
5 small red bliss potatoes,
   cut into quarters
8 ounces green beans,
   trimmed
8 ounces asparagus, trimmed

Combine the olive oil, garlic, rosemary, thyme, salt and pepper in a small bowl and mix well. Place the sweet potatoes, squash, zucchini, potatoes, green beans and asparagus in a large bowl. Add the herb mixture and toss to coat evenly. Place on a rimmed baking sheet. Bake at 375 degrees for 20 to 25 minutes or until the vegetables are tender.

Yield: 8 servings

Creamy Wild Mushroom Bread Pudding

This is good baked in a cleaned 2-pound pumpkin stripped of seeds and pulp. Spoon the bread pudding into the prepared pumpkin and replace the top of the pumpkin. Wipe the outside of the pumpkin with olive oil. Bake on a foil-lined pan at 350 degrees for 45 minutes.

2¹/2 cups (1-inch cubes)
   French bread
1 teaspoon butter, softened
1 tablespoon olive oil
1 cup (¹/4-inch-thick slices)
   portabello mushroom caps
1 cup (¹/4-inch-thick slices)
   shiitake mushroom caps
1 teaspoon finely
   chopped garlic
¹/2 teaspoon fresh
   thyme leaves
¹/2 teaspoon kosher salt
¹/4 teaspoon pepper
4 eggs
1 cup heavy cream

Place the bread cubes on an ungreased baking sheet. Bake at 350 degrees for 10 minutes or until toasted. Remove from the oven to cool. Spread the butter in an 8×8-inch baking dish. Place the bread cubes in the prepared dish. Maintain the oven temperature. Heat the olive oil over medium-high heat in a large skillet. Stir in the portabello mushrooms and shiitake mushrooms. Cook for 3 minutes. Add the garlic, thyme, salt and pepper. Cook for 2 minutes or until the mushrooms are tender. Remove from the heat to cool slightly. Drain the mushrooms in a colander if there is any residual liquid. Beat the eggs in a bowl. Whisk in the cream. Stir in the mushrooms. Pour over the bread cubes, making sure each cube is soaked. Let stand for 5 minutes. Bake for 20 to 25 minutes or until the mixture is set and the bread cubes are golden brown. Let cool for 5 minutes. Cut into squares.

Yield: 6 to 8 servings

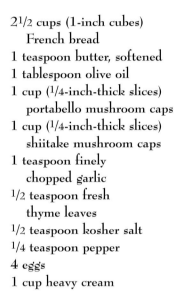

Hot Grilled Grits

1 (10-ounce) can condensed
   chicken broth
1 (8-ounce) jar processed
   cheese spread
1/2 cup water
1/4 cup (1/2 stick) butter
   or margarine
1 tablespoon minced pickled
   jalapeño chiles
1/2 teaspoon salt
1 cup quick-cooking grits
1 tablespoon olive oil
Tomato Salsa (below)

Bring the broth, cheese spread, water, butter, jalapeño chiles and salt to a boil in a large saucepan over medium heat. Stir in the grits. Cover and reduce the heat. Cook for 6 to 8 minutes, stirring frequently. Pour into a lightly greased 9-inch pie plate. Let stand until cool. Unmold the grits and cut into six wedges. Lightly brush each side with the olive oil. Place on a grill rack sprayed with nonstick cooking spray. Grill, covered, over 300- to 350-degree heat for 4 minutes on each side or until golden brown. Serve with Tomato Salsa.

Yield: 6 servings

Tomato Salsa

This is super. It can be served as a main course or appetizer.

4 tomatoes, seeded
   and chopped
2 jalapeño chiles, seeded
   and minced
1/2 cup minced onion
1/3 cup finely chopped green
   bell pepper
4 garlic cloves, minced
2 tablespoons olive oil
1 tablespoon fresh lemon
   juice or lime juice
1/4 cup minced fresh cilantro
1/2 teaspoon oregano
Salt and pepper to taste

Combine the tomatoes, jalapeño chiles, onion, bell pepper, garlic, olive oil, lemon juice, cilantro, oregano, salt and pepper in a bowl and mix well. Chill, covered, until serving time.

Yield: about 5 cups

Mac and Cheese

This Mac and Cheese is a standard one. You can use Brie as a third cheese for a really creamy texture. Everyone loves Mac and Cheese, especially me.

1¹/2 cups (6 ounces) coarsely shredded Gruyère cheese or Swiss cheese

3 cups (12 ounces) coarsely shredded Cheddar cheese

5 tablespoons butter

¹/4 cup all-purpose flour

1 teaspoon fresh thyme leaves

¹/4 teaspoon nutmeg

4 cups milk

16 ounces penne

Salt to taste

1³/4 cups fresh bread crumbs from trimmed French bread

Mix the Gruyère cheese and Cheddar cheese in a large bowl. Melt 4 tablespoons of the butter in a large saucepan over medium heat until the butter bubbles. Whisk in the flour. Cook for 3 minutes or until the mixture bubbles again, whisking constantly. Add the thyme and nutmeg. Whisk in the milk gradually. Simmer for 4 minutes or until thickened and smooth, stirring frequently. Add the cheese mixture. Cook until melted and smooth, stirring constantly. Cook the pasta in boiling salted water in a saucepan until tender but firm to the bite; drain. Place in a large bowl. Add the cheese sauce and toss to coat. Pour into a greased 2-quart baking dish. Melt the remaining 1 tablespoon butter in a large heavy skillet over medium-high heat. Add the bread crumbs and toss to coat. Cook for 2 minutes or until golden brown, stirring constantly. Sprinkle over the pasta mixture. Bake at 375 degrees for 20 minutes or until bubbly.

Yield: 8 to 10 servings

Chocolate Pavlova with Tangerine Whipped Cream

This dessert is spectacular in taste and so beautiful. It's a crowning end to a special feast and worth all the effort.

Tangerine Whipped Cream

1 cup heavy whipping
    cream
2 tablespoons sugar
Finely grated zest of
    1 tangerine

Whip the cream with the sugar in a mixing bowl until firm. Beat in the tangerine zest.

Yield: 1 cup

4 egg whites,
    at room temperature
1/8 teaspoon cream of tartar
1/8 teaspoon salt
1 cup sugar
1 1/2 teaspoons cornstarch
1 tablespoon red
    wine vinegar
1/4 cup unsweetened Dutch-
    processed baking cocoa,
    sifted (3/4 ounce)
Tangerine Whipped Cream
    (at left)
1 1/2 cups fresh fruit,
    such as raspberries,
    sliced strawberries,
    sliced mangoes or
    a mixture of all
3 kiwifruit, sliced into
    half moons

Cut a piece of baking parchment to fit on a baking sheet. Draw a 9-inch circle in the center of the baking parchment with a pencil. Line the baking sheet with the baking parchment with the marked side down. Whip the egg whites, cream of tartar and salt at medium speed in a large dry bowl of a stand mixer fitted with the whisk attachment for 30 seconds or until foamy. Add the sugar gradually, whipping constantly. Whip in the cornstarch and vinegar. Beat for 3 to 5 minutes longer or until stiff, glossy peaks form. Add the baking cocoa. Beat at low speed for 20 to 30 seconds, scraping the bowl as needed. Fold the meringue with a rubber spatula until no streaks of white remain. Spoon the meringue inside the circle on the baking parchment. Spread with a spatula to even out slightly. Bake at 350 degrees on the center oven rack for 10 minutes. Reduce the oven temperature to 300 degrees. Bake for 45 to 50 minutes longer or until the meringue has puffed and cracked around the edge. Turn off the oven. The delicate meringue won't collapse as much if it cools gradually. Place the meringue on a serving platter. Spoon the Tangerine Whipped Cream on the meringue, spreading almost to the edge. Top with the fruit. Cut into wedges with a serrated knife.

Yield: 8 to 10 servings

Pineapple Bread Pudding

*A bourbon sauce just makes a bread pudding. This bread pudding
is exceptionally tasty. If you're in a hurry and want to cheat, stir a few
spoonfuls of bourbon into melted vanilla ice cream and it
mimics a homemade bourbon sauce.*

3¹/2 cups milk
1 large loaf French bread
3 eggs
¹/3 cup sugar
Pinch of salt
¹/4 cup (¹/2 stick)
　butter, melted
1 teaspoon vanilla extract
1¹/2 cups drained crushed
　pineapple
¹/2 cup raisins or
　golden raisins
Grated nutmeg to taste
Bourbon Sauce (below)

Microwave the milk in a 2-quart microwave-
safe glass measure until scalded. Tear the
French bread into small pieces and place in a
large bowl. Beat the eggs, sugar and salt in a
mixing bowl until well mixed. Stir in the
scalded milk and butter. Pour over the bread.
Add the vanilla, pineapple, raisins and nutmeg.
Let stand for 15 minutes. Spoon into a
baking dish. Place in a larger baking dish and
fill with enough hot water to come halfway
up the side of the smaller baking dish. Bake
at 350 degrees for 1 hour or until a knife
inserted in the center comes out clean. Serve
warm with Bourbon Sauce.

Yield: 8 servings

Bourbon Sauce

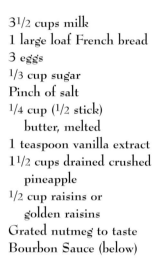

¹/2 cup (1 stick)
　unsalted butter
¹/2 cup packed light
　brown sugar
¹/2 cup granulated sugar
1 egg
3 tablespoons bourbon

Melt the butter, brown sugar and granulated
sugar in a saucepan over low heat until the
sugars dissolve. Whisk the egg in a mixing
bowl. Add a small amount of the hot mixture
to the beaten egg. Stir the egg into the hot
mixture. Cook until the sauce is smooth,
whisking constantly. Do not boil. Whisk in
the bourbon.

Yield: about 2 cups

Coconut-Cream Cheesecake

This was one of our favorites at Johnston Street Café, which I owned for ten years. Pat Owens and Margaret Minton loved it and indulged themselves when we had it available.

2/3 cup all-purpose flour
1 tablespoon sugar
5 tablespoons cold butter,
   cut into small pieces
24 ounces cream cheese,
   softened
1 1/2 cups sugar
4 eggs, at room temperature
2 cups flaked coconut
1 cup whipping cream
1 teaspoon fresh lemon juice
1 teaspoon vanilla extract
1/2 teaspoon almond extract
Toasted flaked coconut
   for garnish

Pulse the flour and 1 tablespoon sugar in a food processor to mix. Add the butter and process until the mixture resembles coarse cornmeal. Shape into a ball and wrap in plastic wrap. Chill for 15 minutes. Press the dough into a springform pan, evenly covering the bottom. Bake at 325 degrees for 15 to 20 minutes or until golden brown. Let cool slightly. Reduce the oven temperature to 300 degrees. Beat the cream cheese and 1 1/2 cups sugar in a mixing bowl until smooth. Beat in the eggs one at a time. Add 2 cups coconut, the whipping cream, lemon juice, vanilla and almond extract and mix well. Pour into the crust. Bake for 1 hour. Let cool on a wire rack. Chill until serving time. Release and remove the side of the pan. Garnish with the toasted coconut. The cheesecake may be made two days ahead and also may be frozen. To toast the coconut, spread in a single layer on a baking sheet and bake at 250 degrees just until the coconut begins to turn brown, watching carefully to prevent overbrowning.

Yield: 8 to 10 servings

Microwave Custard

1 cup sugar
1 teaspoon salt
1/4 cup cornstarch
5 cups milk
8 egg yolks, beaten
4 teaspoons vanilla extract

Mix the sugar, salt and cornstarch in a 2-quart microwave-safe glass measure. Stir in the milk gradually. Microwave on High for 7 minutes or until slightly thickened, whisking every 3 minutes. Stir slightly more than one-half of the hot mixture into the egg yolks. Stir the egg yolks into the hot mixture. Whisk in the vanilla.

Yield: 10 to 12 servings

Lemon Curd

Bill, my husband, in between making rounds at both hospitals, would come in the back door of Johnston Street Café, my restaurant, knowing full well we would have lemon curd, and he would say, "Do you have any lemon curd I can have for lunch?" This was not a healthy lunch, but when he was in a hurry, this was a divine lunch for him.

1 cup (2 sticks) butter
3 cups sugar
8 eggs
1 tablespoon grated
    lemon zest
Juice of 6 lemons

Place the butter in a 2-quart microwave-safe glass measure. Microwave on High at 30-second intervals until the butter is melted. Add the sugar, eggs, lemon zest and lemon juice and mix well. Microwave on High for 4 minutes. Whisk the mixture until smooth. Microwave on Medium for 4 minutes. Whisk until smooth. Microwave for 4 minutes longer. Whisk until smooth. Repeat until the mixture is thick, whisking after each interval. Let stand until cool. Store in the refrigerator.

Yield: about 6 cups

The Microwave Custard, which can be used plain, as a custard for banana pudding, as an anglaise sauce (bourbon can be added), as a custard for a trifle, and for many other uses, is something I made practically every day when I owned Johnston Street Café—what a time saver! I could be working around the kitchen doing other things and then run over and whisk the custard when necessary.

Flan

*This darling lady, Maria Alonzo, in the midst of moving, came
to Decatur to teach the class, "A Salute to Spain." Her paella recipe was
superior, and I was so impressed with her flan recipe—so different
from my recipe, but easier. It truly is a treat.*

1 cup sugar
1 (14-ounce) can sweetened
  condensed milk
1 (8-ounce) can evaporated
  milk
1 cup whole milk
6 eggs
1 tablespoon vanilla extract
Pinch of salt

Place 1/4 cup sugar in each of two 5×9-inch loaf pans. Heat the pans over medium heat until the sugar melts and begins to caramelize, swirling the pans constantly. This process is very quick. Remove from the heat and let stand until cool. Combine the remaining 1/2 cup sugar, sweetened condensed milk, evaporated milk, whole milk, eggs, vanilla and salt in a mixing bowl and beat until blended. Pour evenly over the cooled caramel in each pan. Place the pans in a larger baking pan. Add water to the larger pan to come halfway up the side of the smaller pans. Bake at 350 degrees for 55 to 60 minutes or until a wooden pick inserted in the middle of the flan comes out clean. Invert onto a platter. Pour the caramel from the baking pans over the top of the flan. Decorate as desired with pineapple slices, cherries, sliced peaches or whipped cream.

Yield: 12 servings

Strawberry Tiramisu

I couldn't leave this Tiramisu out, as it would go beautifully with the Italian Dinner if you prefer it over the Panna Cotta.

1¹/2 cups strawberry preserves

¹/3 cup plus ¹/4 cup Cointreau or other orange liqueur

¹/3 cup orange juice

16 ounces mascarpone cheese, at room temperature

1¹/2 cups chilled heavy whipping cream

¹/3 cup sugar

2 teaspoons vanilla extract

1¹/2 pounds fresh strawberries

52 (about) crisp ladyfingers or soft ladyfingers

Whisk the preserves, ¹/3 cup of the Cointreau and the orange juice in a 2-cup glass measure until blended. Blend the mascarpone cheese and 2 tablespoons of the remaining Cointreau in a large bowl. Beat the cream, sugar, vanilla and remaining 2 tablespoons Cointreau in a large bowl until firm peaks form. Stir one-fourth of the whipped cream mixture into the mascarpone mixture to lighten. Fold in the remaining whipped cream mixture. Cut one-half of the strawberries into slices. Spread ¹/2 cup of the preserve mixture in a 3-quart oblong serving dish or a 9×13-inch glass dish sprayed with nonstick cooking spray. Arrange enough of the ladyfingers over the preserve mixture to cover the bottom of the dish. Spoon ³/4 cup of the remaining preserve mixture over the ladyfingers. Spread 2¹/2 cups of the mascarpone mixture over the preserve mixture. Arrange the sliced strawberries over the layers. Continue to layer with the remaining ladyfingers, remaining preserve mixture and remaining mascarpone mixture. Chill, covered, with plastic wrap, for 8 to 10 hours. Slice the remaining strawberries. Arrange over the top of the tiramisu and serve.

Yield: 12 servings

Chocolate-Covered Bananas

Wow, how healthy can you get? Bananas and chocolate combined. Use a skewer instead of a popsicle stick or no stick at all.

Colored sprinkles
  for rolling
8 bananas
2 cups (12 ounces)
  semisweet
  chocolate chips

Cover a sheet of waxed paper with sprinkles. Insert a popsicle stick into one end of each banana. Melt the chocolate chips over low heat in a saucepan. Dip the bananas into the chocolate and roll in the sprinkles to coat. Place in the refrigerator or freezer to cool and harden. Bananas also may be dipped in strawberry yogurt and rolled in granola.

Yield: 8 servings

Free-Form French Apple Tart

Occasionally, I just crave an apple pie or tart. This one is fun and yummy.

1¹/4 cups unbleached
  all-purpose flour
  (6 ounces)
2 tablespoons sugar
¹/4 teaspoon salt
6 tablespoons cold
  unsalted butter, cut into
  ¹/2-inch pieces
4 ounces cold cream cheese,
  cut into ¹/2-inch pieces
2 teaspoons fresh lemon juice
1 to 2 tablespoons ice water
1¹/4 pounds Granny Smith
  apples (about 3 medium)
1¹/4 pounds McIntosh apples
  (about 3 medium)
2 tablespoons fresh
  lemon juice
¹/4 cup plus 2 tablespoons
  sugar
¹/2 teaspoon cinnamon
¹/2 teaspoon nutmeg
1 egg white, lightly beaten

Process the flour, 2 tablespoons sugar and the salt in a food processor for several seconds. Add the butter and cream cheese and pulse until the mixture is sandy and pebble-like in texture. Place in a medium bowl. Sprinkle 2 teaspoons lemon juice and the ice water over the mixture. Fold with a spatula to incorporate the liquid into the flour mixture. Place on a clean dry work surface. Gently press together into a ball and flatten into a rough disk. Chill for 30 minutes or until firm. Roll the dough into a 10-inch circle. Place on a baking sheet lined with baking parchment. Peel the apples. Cut the apples into slices ¹/4 inch thick. Combine the apples, 2 tablespoons lemon juice, ¹/4 cup sugar, the cinnamon and nutmeg in a bowl and toss to mix. Arrange the apple slices in concentric circles over the dough, leaving 1 inch of the dough around the edge. Fill the center with the remaining apples. Fold the outer edge of dough tightly up over the apples and cup with your hands to compress and shape. Brush the dough with the egg white. Sprinkle with the remaining 2 tablespoons sugar. Bake at 400 degrees for 40 minutes or until the crust is deep golden brown and the apples are tender. Let cool on the baking sheet for 5 minutes. Remove the tart from the baking parchment to a wire rack. Let cool for 5 minutes. Serve with vanilla ice cream.

Yield: 8 servings

Clara's Blueberry Pie

5 cups fresh or frozen
   blueberries
3/4 cup granulated sugar
1/4 cup packed brown sugar
1/2 cup all-purpose flour
1/4 teaspoon ground allspice
1/2 teaspoon cinnamon
1/2 tablespoon lemon juice
1/2 tablespoon lemon zest
Perfect Pie Pastry (page 172)
Butter for dotting
1 egg
1 tablespoon water
Cinnamon-sugar for
   sprinkling

Combine the blueberries, granulated sugar, brown sugar, flour, allspice, cinnamon, lemon juice and lemon zest in a large bowl and stir to mix well. Roll one portion of Perfect Pie Pastry on a lightly floured surface into a circle. Fit the pastry into a 9-inch pie plate. Spoon the blueberry mixture into the pastry-lined pie plate and dot with butter. Roll the remaining Perfect Pie Pastry on a lightly floured surface into a circle and cut into 1/2-inch strips. Arrange lattice-fashion over the pie, trimming and fluting the edge. Brush the pastry with a mixture of the egg and water. Sprinkle with cinnamon-sugar. Bake at 400 degrees for 20 minutes. Bake, covered with foil, for 20 minutes longer or until the filling is bubbly. Remove from the oven to cool on a wire rack for 1 hour.

Yield: 8 servings

Joe Propst, my friend who stars, along with Rick and Sheri, in the Wild Game Cooking Class, gave me his mother's blueberry pie recipe. It is delicious, and she was a wonderful lady.

Lemon Chess Pie

These are super to pop in the freezer to save as an emergency dessert or for a friend in need.

6 cups sugar
3 tablespoons all-purpose
  flour
12 eggs, lightly beaten
3/4 cup (1 1/2 sticks)
  butter, melted
3/4 cup grated lemon zest
3/4 cup evaporated milk
3/4 cup lemon juice
1 1/2 teaspoons salt
3 unbaked (9-inch) pie shells

Mix the sugar and flour lightly in a bowl. Add the eggs, butter, lemon zest, evaporated milk, lemon juice and salt in the order listed, beating well after each addition until smooth. Pour into the pie shells. Bake at 375 degrees for 15 minutes. Reduce the oven temperature to 300 degrees. Bake for 35 to 45 minutes longer or until set. Let cool on a wire rack.

Yield: 3 pies

Perfect Pie Pastry

2 cups all-purpose flour
1/2 teaspoon salt
3/4 cup (1 1/2 sticks) cold
  unsalted butter
1/4 cup ice water

Process the flour and salt in a food processor for a few seconds. Add the butter and process until the mixture resembles coarse cornmeal. Add the ice water gradually, processing briefly until the dough begins to hold together. Divide the dough into two equal portions. Wrap each portion in plastic wrap and chill for 30 minutes or longer until ready to use.

Yield: enough pastry for two 9-inch pies or for one 9-inch, 2-crust pie

Chilled Lime Coconut Pie

A special friend, Jan Worthey, shared a special recipe—what a refreshing addition for last-course lovers!

35 vanilla wafers
(about 5 ounces)

1/3 cup dry-roasted
macadamia nuts or
cashews (about 2 ounces)

1/3 cup sweetened
flaked coconut

1/4 cup (1/2 stick) unsalted
butter, melted

1 (15-ounce) can cream
of coconut

2/3 cup plain low-fat yogurt

1/2 cup fresh lime juice

2 teaspoons grated lime zest

3 tablespoons cold water

2 teaspoons unflavored
gelatin

3/4 cup chilled heavy
whipping cream

2 tablespoons
confectioners' sugar

1 lime, thinly sliced
for garnish

Process the vanilla wafers and macadamia nuts in a food processor until finely ground. Combine with the coconut and butter in a medium bowl and stir until mixed. Press into a 9-inch metal or glass pie plate with the side buttered. Freeze, covered, for 30 minutes or up to one week. Bake at 350 degrees for 20 minutes or until the crust is golden brown. Remove to a wire rack to cool completely. Whisk the cream of coconut, yogurt, lime juice and lime zest in a 4-cup glass measure or large bowl until blended. Pour the cold water into a 1-cup heatproof glass measure and sprinkle with the gelatin. Let stand for 5 minutes to soften. Set the cup in simmering water in a saucepan, stirring until the gelatin is dissolved. Whisk into the yogurt mixture. Pour into the baked crust. The filling will reach the top of the crust. Chill for 4 hours or until set. The pie may be prepared one day ahead up to this point. Cover and keep chilled until serving time. To serve, beat the whipping cream and confectioners' sugar in a medium bowl until firm peaks form. Garnish the pie with the whipped cream and lime slices.

Yield: 8 servings

Carrot Cake with Cream Cheese Icing

Judge Sherrie Paler claims this "no stack" carrot cake is very tasty. She demonstrated this cake at our Wild Game Dinner, one of our cooking classes with Rick Paler and Joe Propst.

2 cups all-purpose flour
2 teaspoons baking soda
2 teaspoons cinnamon
1 teaspoon salt
3 eggs
2 cups sugar
1 1/2 cups vegetable oil
2 teaspoons vanilla extract
2 cups shredded carrots
1/2 cup crushed pineapple
1 cup chopped pecans
Cream Cheese Icing (below)

Mix the flour, baking soda, cinnamon and salt together. Beat the eggs and sugar in a mixing bowl until pale yellow. Add the oil and beat well. Add the flour mixture and mix well. Stir in the vanilla, carrots, pineapple and pecans. Spoon into a greased 9×13-inch cake pan. Bake at 325 degrees for 1 hour or until the center is set. Remove from the oven to cool. Spread the Cream Cheese Icing over the cool cake.

Yield: 12 servings

Cream Cheese Icing

1/4 cup (1/2 stick) butter, softened
4 ounces cream cheese, softened
1/2 teaspoon vanilla extract
2 cups confectioners' sugar

Beat the butter and cream cheese in a mixing bowl until creamy. Add the vanilla and confectioners' sugar and beat until smooth.

Yield: about 3 cups

Lemon Pound Cake

My sweet sister Catherine Stainback shared this recipe from the Atlanta area—said to be Bishop Asbury's special cake. Use Meyer lemons if available.

2 cups (4 sticks) butter,
   softened
4 cups sugar
10 extra-large eggs
3 tablespoons fresh lemon
   juice
Zest of 1 lemon
1 tablespoon vanilla extract
4 cups plus 3 tablespoons
   sifted all-purpose flour
Lemon Glaze (below)

All ingredients should be at room temperature. Cream the butter and sugar in a mixing bowl for 5 minutes. Add the eggs one at a time, beating well after each addition. Beat in the lemon juice, lemon zest and vanilla at medium speed. Add the flour a small amount at a time, beating well after each addition. Spoon into a greased and floured 10-inch tube pan. Bake at 325 degrees for 1 1/2 hours or until a wooden pick inserted in the cake comes out clean. Let cool in the pan for 15 minutes. Invert onto a wire rack to cool completely. Spoon Lemon Glaze over the cake while still warm.

Yield: 10 to 12 servings

Lemon Glaze

1 cup confectioners' sugar
Zest of 1 lemon
Juice of 1 lemon

Combine the confectioners' sugar, lemon zest and lemon juice in a bowl and mix well.

Yield: 1 cup

Vanilla

Vanilla is an edible seed pod harvested from a special orchid. Vanilla beans are the dried seed pods from the plant. Most vanilla comes from Madagascar, Tahiti, and Mexico. I adore vanilla and add it to everything from desserts to barbecue sauces. I place vanilla beans from which I have extracted the seeds in my sugar bin, and they flavor my sugar slightly.

Hot Milk Cake

This recipe is easy and delicious. With caramel icing, it is divine. It makes great cupcakes, too.

2 cups all-purpose flour
2 teaspoons baking powder
1/4 teaspoon salt
4 eggs
2 cups sugar
1 cup milk
1/2 cup (1 stick) butter
1 teaspoon vanilla extract

Sift the flour, baking powder and salt together. Beat the eggs in a mixing bowl until thick and pale yellow. Add the sugar gradually, beating constantly. Beat in the flour mixture gradually. Heat the milk and butter in a saucepan just to the boiling point. Stir quickly into the batter. Stir in the vanilla. Pour into two well-greased and lightly floured 8-inch cake pans. Bake at 350 degrees for 20 to 25 minutes or until the layers test done. Let cool in the pan for 10 minutes. Invert onto wire racks to cool completely. Frost with your favorite icing, if desired.

Yield: two 8-inch round cakes

Two-Step Pound Cake

This is so easy, but be sure that the butter is soft. Serve with strawberries and a dollop of whipped cream.

4 cups all-purpose flour
3 cups sugar
2 cups (4 sticks) butter, softened
3/4 cup milk
6 eggs
2 teaspoons vanilla extract

Place the flour, sugar, butter, milk, eggs and vanilla in the order listed in a 4-quart mixing bowl. Beat at low speed with a heavy-duty electric mixer for 1 minute. Scrape down the side of the bowl. Continue to beat at medium speed for 2 minutes longer. Pour into a greased and floured 10-inch tube pan. Bake at 325 degrees for 1 1/2 hours or until a wooden pick inserted in the center comes out clean. Let cool in the pan on a wire rack for 10 minutes. Invert onto a wire rack to cool completely.

Yield: 10 to 12 servings

Shortbread

*Beth and Bill Wallace, my daughter Lisa's in-laws, always
entertain at Christmastime with an open house. My husband, Bill,
makes a pig of himself eating the delicious shortbread.*

1 cup all-purpose flour, sifted
1/8 teaspoon salt
1/8 teaspoon baking powder
1/2 cup (1 stick) butter,
  softened
1/4 cup sifted confectioners'
  sugar
1 teaspoon vanilla extract

Mix the flour, salt and baking powder together
in a small bowl. Process the butter in a food
processor until creamy. Add the confectioners'
sugar, vanilla and flour mixture in the order
listed, processing until blended after each
addition. Place the dough between two sheets
of waxed paper. Roll into a rectangle 1/3 inch
thick. Place on a cookie sheet. Chill long
enough for the dough to become firm. Remove
the waxed paper and cut the dough into
squares or the desired shapes. Place on a shiny
or foil-lined cookie sheet. Bake at 350 degrees
for 15 minutes or until the edges begin to
show color, watching carefully.

Yield: 15 to 20 servings

Crispy Oatmeal Cookies

It is hard to find a good, crispy oatmeal cookie recipe,
and this one "takes the cake."

1 cup shortening
1 cup granulated sugar
1 cup packed brown sugar
2 eggs
1 teaspoon vanilla extract
1 1/3 cups all-purpose flour
1 teaspoon salt
1 teaspoon baking soda
3 cups rolled oats
1/2 cup chopped pecans

Cream the shortening, granulated sugar and brown sugar in a mixing bowl until light and fluffy. Beat in the eggs and vanilla. Add the flour, salt, baking soda, oats and pecans and mix well. Drop by spoonfuls onto a greased cookie sheet. Press the tops lightly with a fork. Bake at 350 degrees for 12 to 15 minutes or until golden brown. Let cool on a wire rack.

Yield: 2 dozen cookies

Cinnamon-Nut Palmiers

Super-duper easy, these are beautiful.

1 (17-ounce) package frozen
    puff pastry sheets, thawed
1/4 cup sugar
1 egg
1 tablespoon water
1/2 teaspoon cinnamon
1/3 cup finely chopped
    pecans or walnuts

Unfold the pastry sheets on a surface sprinkled with 2 tablespoons of the sugar. Roll each sheet into a 12×16-inch rectangle. Beat the egg with the water in a small bowl. Brush the pastry sheets with one-half of the egg mixture. Mix the cinnamon, pecans and remaining 2 tablespoons sugar in a small bowl. Sprinkle over the pastries. Roll each pastry up tightly as for a jelly roll, beginning at the short end. Brush with the remaining egg mixture. Cut each roll into slices 1/2 inch thick. Place 2 inches apart on a lightly greased baking sheet. Bake at 400 degrees for 10 minutes or until golden brown.

Yield: 4 dozen

Appendix

Decorating

When entertaining, your surroundings shouldn't be fussy but as simple as possible so people will feel at ease. Use soft lighting and, of course, candles. Flowers should be simply arranged. Keep flowers below eye level at a seated dinner so people can see each other.

- Fruits and vegetables make wonderful centerpiece materials in attractive bowls or pedestals. Stack pomegranates with a few sliced in half for textures.
- Use small, blooming plants placed in small baskets with moss, and include votives if entertaining at night.
- If you have access to magnolia, cut pretty blossoms or just lay leaves of magnolia down the table. Place votives among leaves, and perhaps curl colored ribbon down the table.
- Wrap a large hosta leaf or banana leaf around the inside surface of a glass vase. Fill the vase so that the leaf is submerged. Place blossoming quince or apple branches in the vase.
- Arrange sugared fruit on a pedestal.
- Place single blossoms in small crystal vases. Line down the center of the table.
- Use a hurricane lamp with candleholder and candle with Jackson vine.
- At Thanksgiving, hollow out a pumpkin for use as a bowl to hold the flower arrangement.

Important Temperatures to Know

Meats:

Rare steak	125° F
Rare roast beef	125° F
Well-done beef	165° F
Roast pork	170° F
Turkey/chicken	190° F
Duck/goose	190° F

Breads:

Proofing yeast	110° F
Most breads	200° F

Wine:

Dry white	47°-54° F
Sweet white	44°-47° F
Young reds	54°-60° F
Mature reds	59°-65° F
Champagne	42°-45° F

Candy:

Soft ball	234°-240° F
Firm ball	244°-248° F
Hard ball	250°-266° F

How Much for How Many

For twenty guests you will need one bar; for fifty you will need two bars. The following amounts are for twenty-guest and fifty-guest parties. You may choose to have more or less of some items depending on your menu.

Wines	20-Guest Party	50-Guest Party
Champagne	3 bottles	6 or 7 bottles
White wine	3 or 4 bottles	6 to 8 bottles
Red wine	4 or 5 bottles	11 or 12 bottles
Sparkling water or mineral water	12 (10-ounce) bottles	24 (10-ounce) bottles

Wine: These estimates are based on consumption of two or three 4-ounce glasses per person over a three-hour period with food.

Chill white wine and Champagne for at least three hours before guests arrive. Open two bottles of red wine 30 minutes before guests arrive. Open additional wine as needed.

Bar Set-Up for 24

Dry white wine	6 bottles	Seltzer	6 liters
Dry red wine	2 bottles	Tonic water	4 liters
Champagne or sparkling wine	6 bottles	Perrier or other mineral water	3 liters
Vodka	1 liter	Ginger ale	2 liters
Scotch	1 liter	Grapefruit juice	1 quart
Single-malt scotch	1 bottle	Cranberry juice	1 quart
Rum	1 bottle	Coca-Cola	1 liter
Kentucky straight bourbon	1 bottle		
Dry fine sherry	1 bottle	*1 bottle = 750 milliliters*	
Dry French vermouth	1 bottle	*unless otherwise specified*	

Food Quantities for Serving 25, 50, and 100 People

Food	25 Servings	50 Servings	100 Servings
Sandwiches:			
Bread	50 slices or 3 (1-pound) loaves	100 slices or 6 (1-pound) loaves	200 slices or 12 (1-pound) loaves
Butter	1/2 pound	3/4 to 1 pound	1 1/2 pounds
Mayonnaise	1 cup	2 to 3 cups	4 to 6 cups
Mixed filling (meat, eggs, fish)	1 1/2 quarts	2 1/2 to 3 quarts	5 to 6 quarts
Mixed filling (sweet fruit)	1 quart	1 3/4 to 2 quarts	2 1/2 to 4 quarts
Lettuce	1 1/2 heads	2 1/2 to 3 heads	5 to 6 heads
Meat, Poultry, and Fish:			
Wieners (beef)	6 1/2 pounds	13 pounds	25 pounds
Hamburger	9 pounds	18 pounds	35 pounds
Turkey or chicken	13 pounds	25 to 35 pounds	50 to 75 pounds
Fish, large whole (round)	13 pounds	25 pounds	50 pounds
Fish fillets or steaks	7 1/2 pounds	15 pounds	30 pounds
Salads and Casseroles:			
Potato salad	4 1/4 quarts	2 1/4 gallons	4 1/2 gallons
Scalloped potatoes	4 1/2 quarts or 1 (12×20-inch) pan	8 1/2 quarts	17 quarts
Spaghetti	1 1/4 gallons	2 1/2 gallons	5 gallons
Baked beans	3/4 gallon	1 1/4 gallons	2 1/2 gallons
Jello salad	3/4 gallon	1 1/4 gallons	2 1/2 gallons

Food	25 Servings	50 Servings	100 Servings
Ice Cream:			
Brick	3$^1/4$ quarts	6$^1/2$ quarts	12$^1/2$ quarts
Bulk	2$^1/4$ quarts	4$^1/2$ quarts or 1$^1/4$ gallons	9 quarts or 2$^1/2$ gallons
Beverages:			
Coffee	$^1/2$ pound and 1$^1/2$ gallons water	1 pound and 3 gallons water	2 pounds and 6 gallons water
Tea	$^1/12$ pound and 1$^1/2$ gallons water	$^1/6$ pound and 3 gallons water	$^1/3$ pound and 6 gallons water
Lemonade	10 to 15 lemons and 1$^1/2$ gallons water	20 to 30 lemons and 3 gallons water	40 to 60 lemons and 6 gallons water
Desserts:			
Watermelon	37$^1/2$ pounds	75 pounds	150 pounds
Cake	1 (10×12-inch) sheet cake 1$^1/2$ (10-inch) layer cakes	1 (12×20-inch) sheet cake 3 (10-inch) layer cakes	2 (12×20-inch) sheet cakes 6 (10-inch) layer cakes
Whipping cream	$^3/4$ pint	1$^1/2$ to 2 pints	3 pints

Index

Index

Index

Index

Index

To order additional copies of

Southern Scrumptious Favorites

write to:

Scrumptious, Inc.
4107 Indian Hills Road
Decatur, Alabama 35603

Be sure to include your name and complete address for return mail.
Make checks payable to Scrumptious, Inc.

For one copy of *Southern Scrumptious Favorites* send:	$24.95
Plus sales tax	1.98
Plus postage and handling	3.00
Total	$29.93

For one copy of *Southern Scrumptious Entertains* send:	$21.95
Plus sales tax	1.98
Plus postage and handling	3.00
Total	$26.93

For one copy of *Southern Scrumptious, How to Cater Your Own Party* send:	$19.95
Plus sales tax	1.80
Plus postage and handling	3.00
Total	$24.75

Visit our Web site at www.scrumptiousinc.com
Order books and products and pay through PayPal.
For volume purchases call 256-353-1897.

About the Author

Betty Brandon Sims majored in Foods and Nutrition at
The University of Tennessee. She is a member of The International
Association of Culinary Professionals; she co-edited *Cotton Country Cooking*
and is the author of *Southern Scrumptious: How to Cater Your Own Party*
and *Southern Scrumptious Entertains*.

Betty is passionate about her family, her cooking, and her community.
She has served on many civic boards.
Betty previously owned Johnston Street Café and Catering.
Currently, she owns Scrumptious, Inc., a food consulting business.
She continues to teach cooking classes, speak, and write.

Mrs. Sims lives in Decatur, Alabama, with her husband, Dr. Bill Sims.
Her family includes daughter Libby Sims Patrick, her husband Carl,
and their son Alex; daughter Sheri Sims Hofherr, her daughter Brandon and
son Finlay; son Bill Sims Jr. (deceased), Bill's widow Tara, and
children Will and Allison; and daughter Lisa Sims Wallace, her husband
Paul, and children Paul Jr. and Sims.